C. S. Lewis And The Blessed Virgin Mary

Uncovering A "Marian Attitude"

Arthur Mastrolia

Fairway Press, Lima, Ohio

C. S. LEWIS AND THE BLESSED VIRGIN MARY

FIRST EDITION
Copyright © 2000 by
Arthur Mastrolia

All rights reserved. No portion of this book may be reproduced or utilized in any form or by any means. electronic or mechanical including photocopying, without permission in writing from the publisher. Inquiries should be addressed to: Fairway Press, 517 South Main Street, P.O. Box 4503, Lima, Ohio 45802-4503.

Scripture quotations are from the *New Revised Standard Version of the Bible*, copyright 1989 by the Division of Christian Education of the National Council of the Churches of Christ in the USA. Used by permission.

Some scripture quotations are from *New American Bible*, © 1987, Catholic Bible Press, Nashville. Used by permission.

ISBN 0-7880-1529-6   PRINTED IN U.S.A.

Dedication

*For my nephew Angelo,
who brings joy to life!*

Nihil Obstat: Johann G. Roten, S.M., Director

Vidimus et approbamus: Bertrand A. Buby, S.M., Revisor

Theodore A. Koehler, S.M., Revisor

Thomas A. Thompson, S.M., Revisor

Dayton (Ohio), *ex aedibus Instituti* "International Marian Research Institute," *et Romae, ex aedibus Pontificiae Facultatis Theologicae Marianum, die VIII, mensis Decembris 1998.*

Table Of Contents

Introduction	7
Chapter One:	
Major Themes In The Writings Of C. S. Lewis	15
Chapter Two:	
The Theological Heritage Of C. S. Lewis:	
Critical Influences On His Thought	31
A. The Anglican "Divines"	33
B. Charles Williams and George Macdonald	45
Chapter Three:	
The Marian Attitude In Christian Theology	59
The Mystery of Our Union with God in Christ via the "Marian Attitude"	62
1. The Early Church's Search for a Marian Attitude	64
2. A Marian Attitude in Recent Magisterial Documents	67
a. *Lumen Gentium* VIII: Of the Blessed Virgin, Mother of God in the Mystery of Christ and of the Church	68
i. Introduction — LG #s 52-54	69
ii. LG #s 55-59: The Function of the Blessed Virgin in the Plan of Salvation	69
b. *Marialis Cultus*	72
c. *Redemptoris Mater*	75
d. *Mulieris Dignitatem*	76
e. The *Catechism of the Catholic Church*	81
i. The Faith of Mary in the Catechism of the Catholic Church	85

Chapter Four:
The Marian Attitude In C. S. Lewis   91
    The Marian Attitude in *Perelandra*   104
    1. An Introduction to "The Space Trilogy"   104
    2. The Concept of Obedience in *Perelandra*   108

Chapter Five:
The "Joy" Of The Magnificat Is The "Joy"
Of C. S. Lewis   129
A. Marian Joy in the Magnificat   130
B. The "Joy" of C. S. Lewis   132
    1. "My Spirit Rejoices in God My Savior"   133
    2. Christian Joy is Mediated Through Nature   135
    3. "Joy" in Apparent Opposites   137

Chapter Six:
The Marian Attitude And The Christian Attitude:
Lewisian Weaknesses And Strengths   149

Bibliography   159

Introduction

In recent years, the life and writings of C. S. Lewis have received a tremendous amount of attention from both Christian scholarship and the reading public. Lewis has recently been called "the twentieth-century's favorite Christian writer."[1] Indeed, in 1996, there were still at least sixty works of C. S. Lewis in publication by at least thirty-five publishing companies in the United States alone![2] Popular interest was in great part sparked by the recent Hollywood re-make of the original British film *Shadowlands*. The author's personal library is housed at the Marion E. Wade Center of Wheaton College in Wheaton, Illinois, which was founded in 1965 for the purpose of setting up a study center for the works of seven popular English writers of Christian literature of the twentieth century.[3] The revitalized interest in Lewis as a writer of Christian apologetic and religious fiction has prompted scholars to re-present Lewis's theology and spirituality to an interested readership as literature rich in Christian tradition and orthodoxy which address issues of vital concern to humankind in the latter part of the twentieth century. The "New York C. S. Lewis Society" sends its monthly Bulletin to over 600 members striving to foster and share an appreciation for the author's works, and although its name implies otherwise, it is in fact an international organization![4]

Clive Staples Lewis was born in 1898 in Belfast, Northern Ireland, to Albert James Lewis and Florence Augusta Hamilton, both members of the Church of England (Anglican). Clive (or "Jack" as he would later re-name himself) had an older brother of three years — Warren Hamilton ("Warnie"). Jack's childhood was a relatively happy one — with a loving family which was concerned about his educational and spiritual development. After the death of his mother Jack followed Warnie in 1908 to the first of a line of English boarding schools, where the genius of C. S. Lewis would find its first encouragement and real development. He won a scholarship to University College in Oxford and began to study Classics in 1917. But it was only a few months later that Lewis once again followed Warnie and left Oxford to join the army, where he would serve until being wounded in France in 1918. After a period of convalescence, he returned to Oxford to continue his studies and was awarded a fellowship in English at Magdalen College. This was the beginning of a long settled life as an English "don," which was upset first by his conversion to Christianity (which he had earlier abandoned) and then much later on by his relationship with an American writer, Joy Gresham, whom he married in 1957 at her hospital bedside, a cancer patient. Joy later succumbed to her illness and died in 1960. Jack himself died some three years later.

The preceding provides a skeletal structure of the full life led by C. S. Lewis, which will be analyzed in a detailed consideration of one of his major works, his autobiography — *Surprised by Joy*, in a later chapter. In between the major life events sketched above, Lewis spent his life reading, writing, teaching, and lecturing. His written works are many and varied — from poetry to literary criticism and from Christian apologetics to popular religious fiction. His works have been grouped into eight somewhat distinct areas: personal, literary history and criticism, religious studies, philosophy, collections of essays, poems, fiction and children's fiction.[5]

C. S. Lewis should indeed be considered a "popular writer" — for that is what he was, and his works continue to appeal to a wide popular audience and not only to a strictly theological, spiritual, or even inspirational audience. This does not mean, however, that Lewis was not a serious theologian — despite the fact that he did not consider himself as such. It is precisely because he has made theological exposition accessible through popular literature that I have chosen to study the theological implications of his spiritual reflection. I am convinced that his writings have had profound spiritual impact on very many people who find in them and in his life story an access to theological truths which they otherwise would not have taken from systematic theological treatises which are more often left for professional theologians to study and interpret.

For these reasons of his continued popularity amongst the reading public, I believe it is essential that theologians become conversant with his thought, in order to validate (or invalidate) him theologically as an influential Christian author of the twentieth century. Because his own pilgrimage to the Christian faith was a reasoned and logical one, and because his writings reflect common life experiences, he is widely received as a modern Christian apologist in a post-Christian era. Lewis was able to address theological truths in a language attractive to the non-professional reader as well as to readers of diverse Christian communities. He only and always wanted to elucidate "mere Christianity."

Many religious authors (especially non-Catholic apologists) are admittedly not willing to be explicit about the role of the Blessed Virgin Mary in the economy of salvation, because there does not exist a broad consensus on that role among the various Christian communions. Lewis was very explicit in his confirmation that this was precisely the reason why he himself would say little about Mary other than asserting the theological presuppositions and implications involved in the virgin birth of Christ. Since Lewis did not consider himself a professional theologian, and because he was not a Roman Catholic, we should not expect to find an explicit Mariology in his works. Instead, what I shall attempt to bring to light is the Marian "attitude" (ethos, principal, dimension) which I have found not only to be present in Lewis's thought, but to be a driving — if unconscious — force in most all of his expositions on the nature of Christianity. I wish to assert that while the content of his works is not mariological, his perception of Christian discipleship is strongly Marian. The challenge of this present endeavor is to highlight precisely this dimension and to verify the presuppositions contained therein by recourse to the generally accepted parameters of mariological thought in an attempt to be able to validly recommend the appreciation of this popular modern author in a Marian perspective. Therein lies the novelty of this enterprise in an otherwise well-studied body of material.

An exhaustive review of the pertinent sources reveals that there has never been an exposition or analysis of a Marian attitude in Lewis's works. This has unfortunately reinforced the misguided impression of many of his readers that Lewis had a typically anti-Marian Protestant bias based on evangelical fundamentalism. Now, while there have been recently published dissertations on the male-female relationship in Lewis's writings, on Lewis's concept of the importance of the feminine, and on his anthropological world-view in general, as noted in the bibliographical section of this work, to date no author has commented systematically on any of the mariological references or implications which his writings contain. Recent research into his theological anthropology has revealed that a major theme of Lewis's fiction is the role of women in relationship to men, God and society.[6] Recently, dissertations have been written which analyze Lewis's use of gender as a metaphor to describe the relationship between humankind and God.[7] But work in this area has been limited to the human issues involved — such as the subordination and inferiority of women to men which some have perceived in Lewis's writings.[8] Others have undertaken a deeper theological study on the relationship of nature to the Supernatural as it is revealed in relationships constituted by gender and sexuality, with sexuality understood as an eternal archetype of gender. A commentator recently wrote, "His (Lewis's) views on these issues lie at the very heart of his vision of the universe, of nature, and of the relations of men and women."[9] While his philosophy of religion and his theological anthropology have been much explored, such is not at all the case for the Marian references which are a part of that anthropology and which form what we will call the ever-important "Marian attitude." This is the task undertaken by the present work, wherein our method of procedure will be both a contextual analysis which will study the heritage and milieu from which Lewis himself proceeds, together with an internal critique of the author's principal theological, religious, and spiritual works from the point of view of the integrity of his theological presuppositions and the overall consistency of his themes. Before his conversion experience (1929), Lewis wrote no specifically religious or theological works. In fact, his first publication, *Spirits in Bondage*: A Cycle of Lyrics, much of which was written while he was convalescing from a war wound in various army hospitals, contains poems which reflect his increasing despair about God and things religious. It was published in England in 1919 when Lewis was just twenty years old. His second publication came in 1926 with the romantic poem *Dymer*, written under the name Clive Hamilton. We can say that during this time, Lewis was mostly interested in the study of English literature and in a philosophy of the cosmic or universal spirit which he believed to lie behind all phenomena. He saw human reason as a participation in this cosmic spirit or cosmic logic. He would therefore not write any definitively theological text until well after his conversion to theism and his acceptance of a personal God. In fact, his (later on) self-admitted "chronological snobbery" — the belief that things supernatural belonged to an earlier and ignorant age — precluded in him any appreciation for what we later see in his writings as the "Marian attitude."

The most well-known of his Christian apologetical and spiritual writings were published after his conversion to Christianity (1931) and span over thirty years beginning with his first popular work *The Pilgrim's Regress* (1933) and ending with his last popular work *Letters to Malcolm: Chiefly on Prayer* (published posthumously in 1964). The theology expounded over these thirty years is recognized to be extremely consistent and, in fact, quite repetitive as far as themes are concerned.[10] Even after the death of his beloved wife Joy, we do not witness any significant change or development in this theological presentation. We find his theological anthropology and the Marian attitude which exists within that anthropology to be amazingly consistent throughout the corpus of his works.

Our own approach of putting Lewis's "Marian attitude" in a clear light will proceed as follows. Chapter One will be a presentation and brief exposition of five of the major themes which Lewis employs in his writing followed by a consideration of his writing style — particularly as employed in his fictional works. This chapter will conclude with a proposal of the way in which we hope to situate a "Marian attitude" in much of his written work. Chapter Two will provide an overview of the theological heritage of the Anglicanism which influenced Lewis's thought, as well as the influence of two of his own admittedly most favorite modern Anglican theologians, in order to see how a Marian attitude would not be foreign to his mind. Here we will briefly explore some of the major Anglican theologians of the seventeenth century — the so-called "Golden Age" of Anglicanism — whose theology influenced the thought of Lewis as a scholar of the history of English Literature. We will also consider the critical influence on his thought of the nineteenth and twentieth century Anglican theologians, George Macdonald and Charles Williams. Chapter Three will consist of a presentation of the "Marian attitude" as it has been expressed in Christian theology. In this chapter, we will attempt a definition of a "Marian attitude" by recourse to some of the earliest teachings of certain Fathers of the Church regarding Mary's role in the history of salvation, supplemented by recent magisterial teachings on Mary as well as recent insights of scriptural exegesis of pertinent Marian texts. Once arrived at a definition of a "Marian attitude," we will, in Chapter Four, apply the definition to certain of the major spiritual and theological works of C. S. Lewis to see the proposed correspondence between this attitude and the attitude which comes out of Lewis's writings. His experience of "joy" was a driving force in Lewis's life. Chapter Five will illustrate how the type of joy which we find in the Lucan Magnificat of the Blessed Virgin Mary resonates well with Lewis's understanding of Christian joy. In the concluding Chapter Six, we will briefly summarize Lewis's major themes and discuss the validity of the claim that a "Marian attitude" is central to his theology and to the Christian spiritual life.

---

1. HarperCollins Publishers edition of Walter Hooper, *C. S. Lewis, A Companion & Guide*. (New York: Harper-Collins Publishers, 1996), cover jacket.

2. *Books in Print*, The Master Reference to Titles, Authors, and Publishers, 1996-97 edition, vol. 3. (New Providence, N. J. : R. R. Bowker, 1996).

3. The Marion E. Wade Center of Wheaton College in Wheaton, Ill., is home to a vast collection of books and papers of Owen Barfield, G. K. Chesterton, C. S. Lewis, George Macdonald, Dorothy L. Sayers, J. R. R. Tolkien, and Charles Williams. Contact: Wheaton College, Wheaton, Ill., 60187-5908.

4. Contact: The New York C. S. Lewis Society, James Como, ed., *CSL: The Bulletin of the New York C. S. Lewis Society*, (Jamaica, N. Y.: York College — CUNY — 11451).

5. Peter Kreeft, *C. S. Lewis: A Critical Essay*. (Front Royal: Christendom College, 1988), pp. 69-70.

6. Susan C. Henthorne, *The Image of Woman in the Fiction of C. S. Lewis*. (New York: State University of New York at Buffalo, Ph.D. Thesis, 1985), cf. Abstract.

7. cf. James M. Deschene, *Joy in a Minor Key: The Mystery of Gender and Sex in the Thought of C. S. Lewis*. (Rhode Island: University of Rhode Island, Ph.D. Thesis, 1990).

   Henthorne, ibid.

   Larry R. Hughes, *The World View of C. S. Lewis Implicit In His Religious Writings*. (Albuquerque: University of New Mexico, Ph.D. Thesis, 1980).

8. For example, cf. Henthorne, ibid.

9. Deschene, ibid., p. ii.

10. On consistency of themes prominent in Lewis's thought, cf. Hughes, ibid., esp. pp. 1-16.

Chapter One
Major Themes In The Writings Of C. S. Lewis

Thirty-six years have passed since the death of C. S. Lewis, and throughout the 1990s his popular religious and fictional writings have continued to enjoy immense popularity the world over, and particularly in English-speaking countries. His works appeal to Christians across the denominational spectrum, because he dedicated all of his writing efforts to highlight those elements of the Christian message which are held in common by Christians everywhere — that which he calls "mere Christianity."

It is in this sense that some would question the validity of the present work since Lewis himself recognized that there is no consensus on doctrine among the churches on the figure of the Blessed Virgin Mary.[1] Prescinding, however, from a debate on particular doctrinal issues, it will be our contention that anyone who wants to establish the parameters of "mere Christianity" — Lewis included — must do so necessarily with a Marian attitude. It will also be our contention that Lewis himself was well aware of this fact, and that his writings are imbued with this attitude.

After a complete immersion into the life history and written works of this twentieth century Christian scholar and author, it would be my hope as well as my firm conviction that Lewis himself would not scoff at this attempt to bring into relief the Marian attitude of his thinking. We will discover this attitude to have been an important part of the Anglican heritage to which he was gradually awakened over the long process of his conversion experience.

The writings of Clive Staples Lewis portray his deeply-held regard for the centrality of the Incarnation in the economy of salvation. This first major theme in his theology he called "The Grand Miracle."[2] His appreciation of the centrality of the Incarnation enables him to perceive that there can exist a continuity between nature and Super-nature as this continuity was made evident in God's assumption of human nature. In this way, he may be regarded as an inheritor of that type of Anglican theology which eventually found expression in the Oxford Movement.[3] Some have wondered whether Lewis's incarnational and sacramental theology would have ever moved him to part from the Anglican Church to join the Roman Church.[4] This seems not to have been probable. During his lifetime, Lewis wanted to do nothing which could be construed to highlight the differences between the credal denominations. In a letter to a Roman Catholic priest with whom he corresponded, Don Giovanni Calabria of Verona, Italy, Lewis writes, "Disputations do more to aggravate schism than to heal it: united action, prayer, fortitude and (should God so will) united deaths for Christ — *these will make us one.*"[5]

As a scholar of Medieval and Renaissance English Literature, but particularly after his conversion, Lewis studied the various literary traditions which have expressed both the popular piety and the formal theology of the Anglican Church since its inception. Being admittedly himself "a very ordinary layman of the Church of England, not especially 'high,' nor especially 'low,' nor especially anything else,"[6] he propounds a beautiful incarnational and sacramental theology in his own works which appeal to a wide range of modern Christian readers. Lewis's writings are filled with categories with which his readers can readily identify, not the least of which is the human person's ability to perceive the presence and activity of God in the coming-together of the remarkable with the unremarkable, the discovery of the profound in the simple, the recognition of the

Divine in human form — the faithful who recognize God in Jesus Christ. Lewis inherits much of his theological style from the literary divines of Anglicanism, and the influence on his thought of two outstanding Anglican theologians of the nineteenth and twentieth centuries, respectively George Macdonald and Charles Williams, is immeasurable. His understanding of the Incarnation — or the "Grand Miracle" — informs all of his religious thinking and thus proves to be the foundation of his overall theology as well as his Marian attitude.

A second of Lewis's major themes is the contention that all of reality is hierarchically ordered, from the supernatural down through the natural planes. As a matter of fact, hierarchy exists in the life of the Trinity inasmuch as, for Lewis, God the Father is, as His Name would suggest, patriarchal! There is a *kenosis* which exists within the Godhead itself, causing the Son to submit in love to the mission imposed upon him by the Father — that is, the Incarnation. On this topic, Lewis has a beautiful reflection in *The Problem of Pain*:

> For in self-giving, if anywhere, we touch a rhythm not only of all creation but of all being. For the Eternal Word also gives Himself in sacrifice; and that not only on Calvary. For when He was crucified He "did that in the wild weather of His outlying provinces which He had done at home in glory and gladness." From before the foundation of the world He surrenders begotten Deity back to begetting Deity in obedience. And as the Son glorifies the Father, so also the Father glorifies the Son.[7]

In the context of this hierarchy, all parts of reality and creation find their proper place. Valid hierarchy exists only when authority and obedience are present. The essence and structure of all rightful natural authority is derived from and reflective of its supernatural archetype. This makes Lewis what he himself calls a "Supernaturalist"[8] — or one who believes that a level of reality exists which is distinct from, more important, than and determinative of all other levels.

A third major theme of Lewis's writings is the placement of his thematic of "Supernaturalism" in a relationship of both discontinuity and continuity with "Naturalism," which, left to itself, would maintain that nothing exists outside the whole of nature, thereby denying true human freedom which the Supernaturalist believes to be grounded in that which is beyond nature. Lewis writes:

> ... no thoroughgoing Naturalist believes in free will: for free will would mean that human beings have the power of independent action, the power of doing something more or other than what was involved by the total series of events. And any such separate power of originating events is what the Naturalist denies. Spontaneity, originality, action 'on its own,' is a privilege reserved for 'the whole show,' which he calls *Nature*.
>
> The Supernaturalist agrees with the Naturalist that there must be something which exists in its own right; some basic Fact whose existence it would be nonsensical to try to explain because this Fact is itself the ground or starting-point of all explanations. But he does not identify this Fact with 'the whole show.' He thinks that things fall into two classes. In the first class we find either things or (more probably) One Thing which is basic and original, which exists on its own. In the second we find things which are merely derivative from that One Thing. The one basic Thing has caused all other things to be. It exists on its own; they exist because it exists. They will cease to exist if it ever ceases to maintain them in existence; they will be altered if it ever alters them.
>
> The difference between the two views might be expressed by saying that Naturalism gives us a democratic, Supernaturalism a monarchical, picture of reality ... And just as, in a democracy, all citizens are equal, so for the Naturalist one thing or event is as good as another, in the sense that they are all equally dependent on the total system of things. Indeed each of them is only the way in which the character of that total system exhibits itself at a particular point in space and time. The Supernaturalist, on the other hand, believes that the one original or self-existent thing is on a different level from, and more important than, all other things.[9]

Lewis's insistence on the necessity of hierarchy in an ordered world does not necessarily imply the restriction of human freedom as much as it guarantees the very possibility of that freedom. The Supernaturalist has a greater appreciation of human freedom than does the Naturalist, because, in the end, the thoroughgoing Naturalist is himself conditioned by and not free from the very "nature" in which he finds himself and outside of which nothing exists. The freedom of the Supernaturalist is grounded in a logic which exists independently of nature, a logic yielding a freedom of choice which is not conditioned by the natural order but rooted in a greater Being (God).

C. S. Lewis loved "obedience." This marks the fourth major theme of his works. He once made the comment, "I was not born to be free — I was born to adore and obey."[10] An oft-quoted passage on obedience as understood by Lewis himself comes from a letter he wrote "To a Lady" in 1940:

> About obedience. Nearly everyone will find himself in the course of his life in positions where he ought to command and in positions where he ought to obey ... Now each of them requires a certain training or habituation if it is to be done well; and indeed the habit of command or of obedience may often be more necessary than the most enlightened views on the ultimate moral grounds for doing either. You can't begin training a child to command until it has reason and age enough to command someone or something without absurdity. You can at once begin training it to obey; that is teaching it the art of obedience as such — without prejudice to the views it will hold later on as to who should obey whom, or when, or how much ... since it is perfectly obvious that every human being is going to spend a great deal of his life in obeying.[11]

We intend to highlight the connection between what C. S. Lewis considered to be an important spiritual attitude (obedience) and the attitude of obedience which Sacred Scripture and the teaching Church attributes to the Blessed Virgin Mary.

The new Catechism of the Catholic Church reiterates the Pauline theme that by His loving obedience to the Father, Christ reversed humankind's disobedience and accomplished the atoning mission of the suffering Servant.[12] In view of the grace offered to humankind through Christ's victory over sin, Mary was able to likewise be obedient to the will of the heavenly Father. The Catechism says of her,

> By her complete adherence to the Father's will, to his Son's redemptive work, and to every prompting of the Holy Spirit, the Virgin Mary is the Church's model of faith and charity. Thus she is a "preeminent and ... wholly unique member of the Church"; indeed, she is the "exemplary realization" (*typus*) of the Church.[13]

It is in this sense that Mary is the quintessential Christian and that her attitude is the quintessential Christian one: openness, receptivity, and obedience to the Divine initiatives as they are experienced by the human person.

Let us now turn to a fifth and final theme in the writings of C. S. Lewis. At the risk of being labeled as a sexist or even a misogynist — which he has both been called by critics[14] — Lewis maintains that the same hierarchy elaborated upon above characterizes the proper masculine-feminine relationship. Lewis defends the validity of this idea in the marriage relationship in the following way:

> ... In Christian marriage the man is said to be the "head." Two questions obviously arise here. (1) Why should there be a head at all — why not equality? (2) Why should it be the man?
>
> (1) The need for some head follows from the idea that marriage is permanent. Of course, as long as the husband and wife are agreed, no question of a head need arise; and we will hope that this will be the normal state of affairs in a Christian marriage. But when there is real disagreement, what is to happen? ... If marriage is permanent, one or other party must, in the last resort, have the power of deciding the family policy. You cannot have a permanent association without a constitution.
>
> (2) If there must be a head, why the man? Well, firstly, is there any very serious wish that it should be

the woman? As I have said, I am not married myself, but as far as I can see, even the woman who wants to be the head of her own house does not usually admire the same state of things when she finds it going on next door ... But there is also another reason; and here I speak quite frankly as a bachelor, because it is a reason you can see from outside even better than from inside. The relations of the family to the outer world — what might be called its foreign policy — must depend, in the last resort, upon the man because he ought to be, and usually is, much more just to the outsiders. A woman is primarily fighting for her own children and husband against the rest of the world. Naturally, almost, in a sense, rightly, their claims override, for her, all other claims. She is the special trustee of their interests. The function of the husband is to see that this natural preference of hers is not given its head. He has the last word in order to protect other people from the intense family patriotism of the wife.[15]

In light of the above, it is no wonder that Lewis has been labeled a misogynist. In the present day, the divorce rate and any number of other sociological factors has forced "headship" upon many single mothers — a headship which — many would argue — had been applicable and practical all along. But whether you subscribe to progressive feminism or advocate, like Lewis did, a traditional patriarchal family structure, upon close evaluation what seems to strike the reader more forcefully in the above quotation is not so much the husband's authority in itself as much as how that authority is an accommodation to the strength of a mother's love, which is, in Lewis's notion of reality, more authoritative than any "power" which a man could wield. I think this is the important sentiment that Lewis wants to convey.

"Masculine" and "feminine" are supernatural archetypes — realities which exist on the supernatural level, the translation of which into the male and female sex on the natural level are but paltry shadows of their supernatural counterparts. This is the Platonism of C. S. Lewis, as we see expressed in the following passage from *Miracles*:

> God is basic Fact or Actuality, the source of all other facthood. At all costs therefore He must not be thought of as a featureless generality. If He exists at all, He is the most concrete thing there is, the most individual, "organized and minutely articulated." He is unspeakable not by being indefinite but by being too definite for the unavoidable vagueness of language. The words *incorporeal* and *impersonal* are misleading, because they suggest that He lacks some reality which we possess. It would be safer to call His *transcorporeal, transpersonal*. Body and personality as we know them are the real negatives — they are what is left of positive being when it is sufficiently diluted to appear in temporal or finite forms. Even our sexuality should be regarded as the transposition into a minor key of that creative joy which in Him is unceasing and irresistible. Grammatically the things we say of Him are "metaphorical": but in a deeper sense it is our physical and psychic energies that are mere "metaphors" of the real Life which is God. Divine Sonship is, so to speak, the solid of which biological sonship is merely a diagrammatic representation on the flat.[16]

The phrase "shadowlands" which has been used to describe this "symbolical" understanding of reality which Lewis presents to us — most popularly in his essay, "The Weight of Glory"[17] — is a phrase first utilized by Lewis in *The Last Battle*, his last book in the *Chronicles of Narnia* series.[18] Commentators have used this phrase to best describe Lewis's ideas about life on earth in relation to life in Heaven.[19] Since the Fall, the archetypical realities of Super-nature have been translated into their earthly counterparts of king and subject, male and female, at the great risk of the ugly subversion of those realities in the world which we call sin. A Lewis scholar writes: "Though hierarchy is the keynote of reality, on a human level it is risky; for human nature, flawed by sin, subverts hierarchy into forms of domination, often totalitarian in their expression."[20] Unfortunately, such abuse of authority has too often characterized the relationship between king and subject and male and female throughout history.

If, then, the hierarchical system works perfectly only outside of history — in God's world, and not inside of history, in our world

— should it not be cast aside as too dangerous for life in the world? Lewis would say no, because the archetypical realities are true, and one must never reject truth. These realities must be striven after by all Christians to whom they have been revealed as truth. The fact that it is possible to live out these realities in this fallen world is evidenced by the lives of Jesus and Mary: Jesus our King who becomes our servant and Mary the virgin who becomes a mother. As we shall see in succeeding chapters, there is an abundant amount of material in the writings of C. S. Lewis — both the fictional works and the systematic works — relating to the masculine and feminine archetypes of reality. As well, we will point out direct references to the Blessed Virgin Mary in many of his apologetic texts on the Christian faith which present her as the archetypical figure of femininity. Worthy of special attention, however, are the implicit allusions to the figure of Mary in the fictional works, especially in the second work of the space trilogy, *Perelandra*.

Having laid out five of his major themes, let us now turn to a consideration of the literary style which Lewis employs, particularly in his fictional works, because by understanding this style, we will better appreciate his major themes as spiritual insights which are reflected in his writing style. While Lewis's most obvious use of the technique of allegory can be found in *The Pilgrim's Regress*, Lewis himself has pointed out that he did not intend all of his fictional works to have allegorical significance — particularly *The Space Trilogy* and the *Chronicles of Narnia*. If they are not allegorical, how might we define Lewis's allusions to the Blessed Virgin Mary in fictional works such as *Perelandra*? In these works, Lewis employs a unique style. We are tempted to call it an anagogical style. The difference between allegory and anagogy is quite significant. The author of allegory intends for his characters to represent by their words and behavior certain figures recognizable to the reader. In this way, allegory attempts to teach or convey some truth about actual persons or subjects through the use of literary persons or subjects created by the author. A literary dictionary defines "allegory" in literature as "an extended metaphor in which character, objects, incidents, and descriptions carry one or more sets of fully developed meanings in addition to the apparent and literal ones."[21] The very subject of Lewis's scholarship, Medieval and Renaissance English literature, is filled with allegory, among the most well-known being Spenser's *Faerie Queene* (1590-96). John Bunyan's classic allegorical tale *Pilgrim's Progress* (1678-84) is obviously the very inspiration for Lewis's own *The Pilgrim's Regress*, which Lewis subtitles "An Allegorical Apology for Christianity, Reason and Romanticism." "Anagogy," on the other hand, may be defined as "An elevation of the mind to things celestial. Specifically, the term is used to refer to exegesis that gives a mystical or spiritual meaning or application to the words of the Bible, as opposed to their literal, moral, or allegorical interpretation."[22] Now this "elevation of the mind" need not be a conscious elevation by the author; it may perhaps be a gifted elevation of which the author is not aware at the time. Lewis utilized an anagogical style in the creation of the Naria chronicles and the space trilogy. In the Foreword to Paul F. Ford's book *Companion to Narnia*, Madeleine L'Engle tells us that the four senses of the reading of Scripture (described by St. Thomas Aquinas in his *Summa Theologica*, First Part, question one, article ten) can also be found in true fantasy. She writes:

> The literal level is the story itself. The moral level is what the story has to say ...
> ... For quite a while I struggled to understand the difference between the allegorical level and the anagogical level. Finally it came to me that allegory is simile; this is *like* this. But an anagoge is metaphor; this *is* this; it contains within it something of that which it is trying to express ...
> The anagogical level, I am convinced, is never conscious when it is there, it is sheer gift of grace; the writer cannot strive for it deliberately for that would be to ensure failure.
> So I understand Lewis's protestations that he is not writing allegory; of course he isn't. Nevertheless, there is an allegorical level to his stories, and, when he is at his best, an anagogical level ...
> It doesn't bother me at all that Lewis was convinced that he did not allegorize at all in *The Chronicles of*

Narnia. When a writer opens up to a fantasy world, a world which has more depths of reality to it than the daily world, all kinds of things happen in his stories that he does not realize ... If grace comes during the writing of fantasy, the writer writes beyond himself, and may not discover all that he has written until long after it is published, if at all.[23]

If anagogy "contains within it something of that which it is trying to express," then it is symbolic literature in the highest sense of the term "symbol." The figures in anagogical literature do not merely "stand for" the reality which they are trying to represent (this would be allegory); rather and more importantly, they "participate in" the reality which they are meant to represent. On this distinction between allegory and symbolism, Lewis writes in *The Allegory of Love*:

> On the one hand you can start with an immaterial fact, such as the passions which you actually experience, and can invent *visibilia* to express them. If you are hesitating between an angry retort and a soft answer, you can express your state of mind by inventing a person called *Ira* with a torch and letting her contend with another invented person called *Patientia*. This is allegory, and it is with this alone that we have to deal. But there is another way of using the equivalence, which is almost the opposite of allegory, and which I would call sacramentalism or symbolism. If our passions, being immaterial, can be copied by material inventions, then it is possible that our material world in its turn is the copy of an invisible world. As the god Amor and his figurative garden are to the actual passions of men, so perhaps we ourselves and our 'real' world are to something else. The attempt to read that something else through its sensible imitations, to see the archetype in the copy, is what I mean by symbolism or sacramentalism. It is, in fine, 'the philosophy of Hermes that this visible world is but a picture of the invisible, wherein, as in a portrait, things are not truly but in equivocal shapes, as they counterfeit some real substance in that invisible fabrick.' The difference between the two can hardly be exaggerated. The allegorist leaves the given

25

— his own passions — to talk of that which is confessedly less real, which is a fiction. The symbolist leaves the given to find that which is more real.[24]

In this way, in *The Chronicles of Narnia*, Aslan stands "as" Christ, albeit in a different reality and in a different world.[25] This understanding of Lewis's style allows Ford to write:

> Lewis would agree that the best way to appreciate a story is to step into it and enjoy it ... Stories are living things; and the result of any vivisection is only data about the thing and not the thing itself ... Another hazard to be avoided is the desire to look for allegories, one-to-one correspondences between philosophical or religious concepts and the characters or events or objects in a story. Lewis was adamant that he was not writing allegory when he wrote *The Chronicles*.[26]

This is precisely the reason why I am not concerned to find a plethora of either direct or allegorical references to the *person* of the Blessed Virgin Mary in either the apologetical systematic works of C. S. Lewis or in his popular fiction. Lewis did not want to make allegorical references to the *person* of the Blessed Virgin Mary because, as we stated at the outset, there is no consensus on doctrine among the Churches related to the person of Mary and those without a particular devotion to her might not be receptive to Lewis's writings if they perceived in them direct devotional references to her person. I am much more concerned with locating in Lewis a "Marian attitude" which an anagogical understanding of his fiction will permit and which we find consistently throughout his systematic works. It is an attitude which, for Lewis, exists in the God-head or in the life of the Trinity and which therefore can and should also exist in the life of every Christian initiated into divine life at Baptism.

Why, then, call it a "Marian" attitude? Why not call it simply and more essentially "Christ's" attitude? I say so because, given the Scriptural data, it is as uniquely a Marian attitude as it is Christ's own attitude — Mary having freely embraced in her humanity the attitude that was Christ's.[27] In this way, Mary is to the Church what the spotless Church is to the world: a perfect example of how redeemed human life is supposed to be lived. In her person, humankind's participation in the attitude of the God-man is brought into high relief. This participation is defined as something essentially feminine and uniquely Marian.[28] Mary's mode of participation in the economy of salvation — obedience to the will of God, openness and receptivity to the Divine initiatives in her life — must be the mode of participation of all Christians. This Marian attitude is essential to the full realization of the "joy" of the *Magnificat* — the paradoxical joy that is to be found in the raising of the lowly to high places and in the Incarnation of the Word. It is what Cardinal Joseph Ratzinger has called "joy in the Word become man, the dance before the Ark of the Covenant, in self-forgetful happiness, by one who has recognized God's salvific nearness. Only against this background can Marian devotion be comprehended."[29]

---

1. C. S. Lewis, *Mere Christianity*. (New York: The Macmillan Company, 1952), p. vii.

2. _____, *Miracles, A Preliminary Study*. (New York: The Macmillan Company, 1947), pp. 108-31.

3. A. M. Allchin, *The Joy of All Creation*, An Anglican Meditation on the Place of Mary. (Cambridge, MA: Cowley Publications, 1984), p. 99.

4. Christopher Derrick, *C. S. Lewis and the Church of Rome*. (San Francisco: Ignatius Press, 1981).

5. C. S. Lewis, *Letters to Don Giovanni Calabria, A Study in Friendship*, translated and edited by Martin Moynihan. (London: Collins, 1988), p. 39.

6. C. S. Lewis, *Mere Christianity*, p. vi.

7. C. S. Lewis, *The Problem of Pain*. (New York: The Macmillan Company, 1945), p. 140.

8. C. S. Lewis, *Miracles, A Preliminary Study*, pp. 5-11.

9. Ibid., pp. 7-8.

10. As quoted in the essay "About Anthroposophy" by A. C. Harwood in *C. S. Lewis at the Breakfast Table and Other Reminiscences*, James T. Como, ed. (New York: Harcourt-Brace, 1992), p. 29.

11. *Letters of C. S. Lewis*, Edited, with a Memoir, by W. H. Lewis (London: Geoffrey Bles, 1975), p. 179.

12. *Catechism of the Catholic Church.* (New York: William H. Sadlier, Inc., 1994), #s 615 & 623.

13. Ibid., #967.

14. Susan C. Henthorne, *The Image of Woman in the Fiction of C. S. Lewis.* (New York: State University of New York at Buffalo, Ph.D. Thesis, 1985).

15. C. S. Lewis, *Mere Christianity*, pp. 87-88.

16. C. S. Lewis, *Miracles*, p. 91.

17. C. S. Lewis, *The Weight of Glory and Other Addresses.* (New York: Macmillan Publishing Company, 1980), pp. 3-19.

18. C. S. Lewis, *The Last Battle*, Book Seven in *The Chronicles of Narnia.* (New York: HarperCollins Publishers, 1956), p. 210.

19. cf. Peter Kreeft, *The Shadow-Lands of C. S. Lewis*, (San Francisco: Ignatius Press, 1994), esp. pp. 15.

20. James M. Deschene, *Joy in a Minor Key: The Mystery of Gender and Sex in the Thought of C. S. Lewis.* (Rhode Island: University of Rhode Island Doctoral Dissertation, 1990), pp. ii-iii.

21. *Benet's Reader's Encyclopedia.* (New York: Harper and Row, Publishers, Inc., 1987), p. 25.

22. Ibid., p. 33.

23. Madeleine L'Engle, "Foreword" in *Companion to Narnia* by Paul F. Ford (San Francisco: HarperCollins Publishers, 1994), pp. xii-xv. Here, L'Engle is referring to Lewis's comment in the preface to *Perelandra* that "All the human characters in this book are purely fictitious and none of them is allegorical."

24. C. S. Lewis, *The Allegory of Love*. (New York: Oxford University Press, 1958), pp. 44-5.

25. The conviction that he was not allegorizing in *The Chronicles of Narnia* comes from a number of letters written by Lewis, among them this one to a Mrs. Hook:
    In reality, he (Aslan) is an invention giving an imaginary answer to the question, 'What might Christ become like if there really were a world like Narnia and He chose to be incarnate and die and rise again in *that* world as He actually has done in ours?' This is not allegory at all ... The Incarnation of Christ in another world is mere supposal; but *granted* the supposition, He would really have been a physical object in that world as He was in Palestine and His death on the Stone Table would have been a physical event no less than His death on Calvary. [*Letters of C. S. Lewis*, W. H. Lewis, ed. (New York: Harcourt, Brace and World, 1966), p. 283.]

26. Ford, *Companion to Narnia*, ibid., p. xxv.

27. cf. Philippians 2:5.

28. cf. C. S. Lewis's essay *"Priestesses in the Church?"* in *God in the Dock, Essays on Theology and Ethics*, edited by Walter Hooper. (Grand Rapids, Michigan: Eerdmans, 1970), especially pp. 235-6: "All salvation depends on the decision which she made in the words *Ecce ancilla*; she is united in nine months inconceivable intimacy with the eternal Word; she stands at the foot of the cross" and p. 239 where Lewis is describing the nature of the relationship of the Church of God: "for we are all, corporately and individually, feminine to Him."

29. Joseph Cardinal Ratzinger, *Daughter Zion*. (San Francisco: Ignatius Press, 1983), p. 82.

Chapter Two
The Theological Heritage Of C. S. Lewis: Critical Influences On His Thought

It is important for us now to consider the theological context out of which C. S. Lewis comes and from which he elaborates the major themes referred to in the first chapter. This needs to be done in order to see how the most important influences on the theological mind of C. S. Lewis permit him, as we shall see, to hold the place of the Blessed Virgin Mary in the economy of salvation in high esteem. Lewis staunchly maintained and defended certain basic Christian truths which he believed to be at the center of the major Christian communions.[1] He was particularly interested to defend the Incarnation — which he called "The Grand Miracle,"[2] the Virgin Birth,[3] and the bodily resurrection of Jesus.[4] He tells us quite admittedly how basic Christian doctrine was most impressed on his mind at his childhood boarding school (which he mockingly referred to as "Belsen," a Nazi death camp!) in Hertfordshire, England:

> There first I became an effective believer. As far as I know, the instrument was the church to which we were

taken twice every Sunday. This was high 'Anglo-Catholic.' On the conscious level I reacted strongly against its peculiarities — was I not an Ulster Protestant, and were not these unfamiliar rituals an essential part of the hated English atmosphere? Unconsciously, I suspect, the candles and incense, the vestments and the hymns sung on our knees, may have had a considerable, and opposite, effect on me. But I do not think they were the important thing. What really mattered was that I here heard the doctrines of Christianity (as distinct from general "uplift") taught by men who obviously believed them. As I had no skepticism, the effect was to bring to life what I would already have said that I believed. In this experience there was a great deal of fear. I do not think there was more than was wholesome or even necessary; but if in my books I have spoken too much of Hell, and if critics want a historical explanation of the fact, they must seek it not in the supposed Puritanism of my Ulster childhood but in the Anglo-Catholicism of the church at Belson.[5]

Though he was indeed an Ulster Protestant, any prejudice which Lewis might have had against the "high" side of the Church of England was not theological. In fact, what we will see in Lewis is a great appreciation for the theology of seventeenth-century Anglicanism — called the "Golden Age" of Anglican theology because of the teachings and writings of the so-called Anglican "divines" such as Richard Hooker, George Herbert, Lancelot Andrewes, Jeremy Taylor, Thomas Traherne and others. These remained true to their own theological heritage which stood in "continuity with the Church of the centuries before the Reformation" while being indebted "to certain of the central affirmations of the Reformers, men who sought to enlarge and deepen that faith and life through a contact with the living tradition of the Fathers of the church, particularly those who lived before the split between East and West."[6] At the same time, they somewhat preserved themselves from the vitriolic prejudices of the reformers like Luther and Calvin. Their influence will be important for Lewis's understanding of the centrality of the Incarnation in theology and the place of the Blessed Virgin Mary in the economy of salvation.

In addition, the influences on Lewis's theology of two, more contemporary, Anglican authors cannot be underestimated. These were George Macdonald (1824-1905) and Charles Williams (1886-1945). It was in reading and re-reading Macdonald's book *Phastastes, A Faerie Romance*,[7] that Lewis began to return, after a long period of atheism, to the idea of the "Holy."[8] As a member of the "Inklings" — that famous group of Oxford dons and others who met regularly for "merriment, piety, and literature"[9] from roughly 1939-1945 — Lewis was in the good company of Charles Williams, a poet and theological writer who did much "to commend Christianity in a Catholic and sacramental form to many who would have been unmoved by conventional apologetic."[10] In the published *Letters of C. S. Lewis*, no other figure does Lewis more often praise for his writing and theological reflection than his "friend of friends"[11] Charles Williams. Lewis recognized in Williams a "direct appeal which disregards the contemporary climate"[12] and a purveyor of Christian faith par excellence.[13] Though there were other ancient, medieval, and contemporary authors and friends who influenced Lewis's way of thinking (like Plato, Dante, George Herbert, Owen Barfield, J. R. R. Tolkien, Hugo Dyson[14]), none seemed to have more consistent impact than the Divines, Macdonald, and Williams. We shall find that the influence of the Divines and Williams falls particularly upon Lewis's theology of the Incarnation and the continuity of Nature and Supernature, while Williams also greatly contributes to Lewis's understanding of the relationship of the Natural to the Supernatural and the masculine and feminine archetypes of reality. Macdonald has his influence on Lewis on the thematics of hierarchy and obedience.

A. The Anglican "Divines"

The Anglican divines were the foremost theologians and advocates of the Anglican Church in the latter half of the sixteenth and throughout the seventeenth centuries. Besides their theology, they are also distinguished for the elegant English prose and poetry with which they conveyed their teachings. In his autobiography, Lewis mentions the influence of the English poet and divine George Herbert (1593-1633), whom he was reading just before his own conversion which occurred after his days as a student and in the second year of his professorial career at Magdalen College in Oxford. Lewis reminisces about reading English literature during his fourth year (1922) as a student at Oxford:

> Now that I was reading more English, the paradox began to be aggravated. I was deeply moved by *The Dream of the Rood*; more deeply still by Langland; intoxicated (for a time) by Donne; deeply and lastingly satisfied by Thomas Browne. But the most alarming of all was George Herbert. Here was a man who seemed to me to excel all the authors I have ever read in conveying the very quality of life as we actually live it from moment to moment, but the wretched fellow, instead of doing it all directly, insisted on mediating it through what I would still have called "the Christian mythology."[15]

What was it in Herbert that attracted Lewis? The Anglican Church in the first part of the seventeenth century was seeking to define itself theologically, ecclesiologically, and spiritually in the post-Reformation period of the seventeenth century. Herbert, like the other divines, preferred to see the Anglican Church situated in a long tradition of Christianity, unrestricted by the sixteenth century controversies and prejudices to which the Reformation gave rise. Commenting on the efforts of the seventeenth century divines to highlight the essentials of the faith (the Incarnation, the Virgin Birth, the salvific nature of Christ's life, and the Christian person's subsequent participation in that life) rather than matters of lesser importance, the Anglican theologian A. M. Allchin writes in his preface to a modern publication of Herbert's works, "Much of this (the 'essentials'), too, we find in Herbert with the intensely Christocentric quality of his thought and devotion, and his remarkable capacity to hold together things often believed to be separable or opposed to one another."[16] For Herbert, as for Lewis, the Incarnation is at the heart of all theology. Allchin continues:

> So alike in his poetry and his prose Herbert discovers the sacramental quality of all life, of the whole creation ... All things share in God's life. We are reminded of Hooker's great assertion, 'All things that are of God (and only sin is not) have God in them and he them in himself likewise.' All things may be known as ways in which God comes to us and speaks with us. Nothing is excluded.[17]

As noted above, Lewis was attracted by Herbert's ability to appreciate the quality of life as it is lived from moment to moment. The fact that Herbert attributed the sacredness of all reality to the mystery of the Incarnation as well as the fact that all reality (except sin) has sacramental value was something which Lewis would only fully appreciate after his conversion. Nevertheless, there was something in Herbert, despite what Lewis then characterized as his "Christian mythology," which Lewis identified as having depth and richness. In comparison with other authors of the same period as Herbert, Lewis says "On the other hand, most of the authors who might be claimed as precursors of modern enlightenment seemed to me very small beer and bored me cruelly."[18] We shall see the influence of Herbert's appreciation of the sacramental value of creation in the theology of Lewis, which theology portrays a rich understanding of the continuity that exists between worldly reality and the supernatural reality which it springs from and in which it is destined for fulfillment. Commenting on Platonic dualism, Lewis writes, "Nature, the phenomenal world, is in Plato's dualism a copy of the real and supersensuous world. Dialectic leads us up from unreal Nature to her real original."[19] He describes this "dialectical continuity" with varied images throughout his writings and we will study this theme of the continuity between nature and super-nature in detail in the next chapter.

An appreciation of the value of image, symbol, or sacrament is surely a part of the Anglican theological heritage of the literary divines. Numerous historians of Anglican theology will bear witness to this fact.[20] In a very recent work entitled *Christ the Self-Emptying of God*, we find an evaluation of the poetic imagery of George Herbert in light of Karl Rahner's understanding of "symbolic reality," which states that "All beings are by their nature symbolic, because they necessarily 'express' themselves in order to attain their own nature."[21] Since the principle of "kenosis" or self-emptying is at the heart of all true self-expression, the author concludes that the kenotic theological poetry of George Herbert, who believed, as explained above, that all reality (except sin) has sacramental value, is among the most purely symbolic or expressive poetry in all of the English language:

> Other than William Tyndale's Englishing of Philippians 2:5-11, in 1526, the purest kenotic poetry in English is that of George Herbert, simultaneously characterized by power and powerlessness, magisterial in its rhetorical command (Herbert had been Public Orator to the University of Cambridge), and yet recurrently and finally self-humbling ...[22]

In the Incarnation, the Word humbled itself to be thoroughly united with humanity and the natural world — thereby sanctifying that natural world through the Word's kenosis and making the world and all of nature capable of symbolizing the divine itself!

Though a scholar of the history of English literature, Lewis was not necessarily immersed in the writings of the seventeenth century divines. As a matter of fact, it was not until the Summer of 1931, six years after he began teaching on the English faculty at Magdalen College, that Lewis was given a copy of the works of two of the divines (Richard Hooker and Jeremy Taylor) by his childhood friend Arthur Greeves. Lewis went on to study these authors in some detail, for he devotes a section of his critical work *English Literature in the Sixteenth Century Excluding Drama* to the writings of Richard Hooker.[23] In the same work, he gives evidence of an intimate knowledge of the other Anglican divines as well, as we shall see below. It is interesting to note that Lewis admits to his conversion to Christianity shortly after having received this gift from Arthur Greeves. Lewis's appreciation of and need for the solid theology of at least some of the Anglican divines is attested to by an important statement quoted by his earliest biographers:

> The truth is that Lewis never got on well with purely devotional books. What he infinitely preferred were solid works of theology that he had to work at to understand. His attitude towards the two kinds of books is summed up in a preface he wrote some years later for a translation of St. Athanasius's *The Incarnation of the Word of God*: 'For my own part I tend to find the doctrinal books often more helpful in devotion than the devotional books, and I rather suspect that the same experience may await others. I believe that many who find that 'nothing happens' when they sit down, or kneel down, to a book of devotion, would find that the heart sings unbidden while they are working their way through a tough bit of theology with a pipe in their teeth and a pencil in their hand.' He must have said as much to Greeves because, when Lewis was on holiday in Ulster during August, 1931, he was presented with the works of the sixteenth- and seventeenth-century Anglican divines, Richard Hooker and Jeremy Taylor.[24]

The most influential Anglican theologians of the post-Reformation period struggled to establish their Anglican identity in a *via media* between the pre-Reformation Church and the anti-Roman sentiments of both the Reformers and the English nationalists. Herbert and others found a way to do this by a return to the theological formulations and expressions of the early Christian communities. Commenting on Herbert's most famous prose work, *The Country Parson*, Allchin writes:

> Here as in other places in Herbert's writing the dichotomies of Evangelical and Catholic are transcended. The affirmations are wholly Catholic because wholly evangelical, wholly evangelical because wholly Catholic. Here is no disjunction of word and sign, of inner and outer, but rather a steadfast attempt to hold them together in a rich if precarious fullness.[25]

As noted in the Introduction, Lewis wanted, in his apologetical works, to say or do nothing that would enhance the breach between the credal denominations. Therefore, Lewis finds himself at home with the *via media* theology of the Anglican divines in his attempts to express "mere Christianity." We find references to his appreciation of the theology of the Anglican divines throughout his autobiographical works.[26]

Let us consider an example of the seventeenth-century Anglican appreciation of the faith reality of the Incarnation and the place of Mary in that mystery. In a poem of George Herbert entitled "To All Angels and Saints," we find peculiar Marian reference which gives us insight into a desire on the part of traditional Anglicanism to engage in Marian devotion — a desire, however, that is checked by the Reformation stance against Marian abuses attributed to the Roman Church. Following is the text of this poem:

Oh glorious spirits, who after all your bands
See the smooth face of God, without a frown
   Or strict commands;
Where ev'ry one is king, and hath his crown,
If not upon his head, yet in his hands:

Not out of envy or maliciousness
Do I forbear to crave your special aid:
   I would address
My vows to thee most gladly, blessed Maid,
And Mother of my God, in my distress.

Thou art the holy mine, whence came the gold,
The great restorative for all decay
   In young and old;
Thou art the cabinet where the jewel lay:
Chiefly to thee would I my soul unfold:

But now (alas!) I dare not; for our King,
Whom we do all jointly adore and praise,
   Bids no such thing:
And where his pleasure no injunction lays,
('Tis your own case) ye never move a wing.

All worship is prerogative, and a flower
Of his rich crown, from whom lies no appeal
   At the last hour;
Therefore we dare not from his garland steal,
To make a poesy for inferior power.

> *Although then others court you, if ye know*
> *What's done on earth, we shall not fare the worse,*
>   *Who do not so;*
> *Since we are ever ready to disburse,*
> *If anyone our Master's hand can show.*[27]

Herbert's emphasis on the centrality of the Incarnation prompts him to express this decidedly reserved if not, in his mind, prohibitive devotion to the one who played an essential role in the mystery of the Word made flesh — the Blessed Virgin Mary. If not for his recognition of the primacy of Jesus' kingship, Herbert says that he would "unfold his soul" unto Mary. Perhaps Lewis read and was influenced by these verses written by one who had made such a deep impression on him.

In 1954, Lewis published his 1944 Clark Lectures given at Trinity College, Cambridge, under the title *English Literature in the Sixteenth Century Excluding Drama*.[28] In this, we have a number of indications of Lewis's extensive familiarity with and appreciation of the Anglican theology of the "Golden Age." As cited above, Lewis devotes a number of pages to the theology and ecclesiology of Richard Hooker (c. 1554-1600), one of the most accomplished apologists and advocates of Anglicanism. These pages give us insight into Lewis's appreciation of Hooker's philosophical and theological views. Hooker developed his doctrine in his monumental *Treatise on the Laws of Ecclesiastical Polity*.[29] In it, he opposes the absolute fundamentalism of the Puritans regarding a literal following of the Scriptures and he elaborates a theory of law based on the supremacy of natural law in the light of which even Scripture must be interpreted. The Church is understood as an organic and not a static reality and room is left for the development of law and doctrine. In this way, the Church of England, he taught, can be seen to be in continuity even with the medieval Church.[30] In *English Literature in the Sixteenth Century Excluding Drama*, Lewis applauds Hooker's stand against the Puritans when he calls him a "far stronger champion" (than the Puritans) on the Anglican side.[31] He quotes Hooker's line about salvation for Roman Catholics: "God, I doubt not, was merciful to save thousands of them."[32]

Let us now examine Lewis's evaluation of this preeminent Anglican divine as found in his critique of Hooker's *Polity in English Literature in the Sixteenth Century.* Lewis points out what he considers to be two main elements in Hooker's thought. The first is this:

> He (Hooker) feels as his deepest enemy what I have called the 'Barthianism' of the puritans, the theology which set a God of inscrutable will 'over against' the 'accursed nature of Man' with all its arts, sciences, traditions, learning, and merely human virtues. In the light of that ruthless antithesis there was only one question to be asked about any institution. Is it 'of God?'; then fall down and worship: is it 'of Man?'; then destroy it. Hooker is always insisting that the real universe is much more complex than that.[33]

The second element of Hooker's thought which Lewis most appreciated was the following:

> Hooker had never heard of a religion called Anglicanism. He would never have dreamed of trying to 'convert' any foreigner to the Church of England. It was to him obvious that a German or Italian would not belong to the Church of England, just as an Ephesian or Galatian would not have belonged to the Church of Corinth. Hooker is never seeking for 'the true Church,' never crying, like Donne, 'Show me deare Christ thy spouse.' For him no such problem existed. If by 'the Church' you mean the mystical Church (which is partly in Heaven) then, of course, no man can identify her. But if you mean the visible Church, then we all know her. She is 'a sensibly known company' of all those throughout the world who profess one Lord, one Faith, and one Baptism.[34]

More than developing a specifically Anglican theology, the Anglican divines were concerned with the development of a theological method. Obviously, Hooker valued human nature much more than his Puritan counterparts. He saw human nature as the seat of an implanted wisdom or reason, the appeal to which, together with

Scripture and universal tradition, constitute the Anglican theological method that he began to develop. One commentator wrote, "The key to Hooker's thought is to be found in the idea that law is an implanted directive, that it is reason, inherent, governing the universe, an inner principle expressing itself by the fulfillment of proper ends."[35] Lewis seems to have taken his philosophy of what he called the "Tao," or the natural law — "the doctrine of objective value, the belief that certain attitudes are really true, and others really false, to the kind of thing the universe is and the kind of things we are"[36] — from Hooker's concept of natural law, as Lewis describes it:

> For explicit divine injunction, embodied in Scripture, is but 'a part of that rule' which we were created to live by (vii. xi. 10). There is another part, no less God-given, which Hooker calls 'nature' (Pref. vi. I), 'law rational, which men commonly used to call the Law of Nature' (I. viii. 9), 'the light of Reason' (I. viii. 3). The most permanent value of Hooker's work lies in his defence of that light.[37]

Lewis, a modern-day apologist who used reason to expound religion and the faith, found many useful insights in Hooker who built a theological method for rational religion and who held reason to be itself an important factor in theology.

Lewis points to Hooker's firm belief in the universality of the Church of Christ. He describes Hooker's position as follows:

> In this Church we have always been and still are. We have not left her by reforming ourselves, nor have the Papists left her by their corrupt 'indisposition' to do likewise (III. i. 10). No doubt many of the questions which Hooker treats are what we should now call questions between 'denominations.' But that is not how he envisages the matter. He is not, save accidentally, preaching 'a religion;' he is discussing the kind and degree of liberty proper to national churches within the universal, visible Church.[38]

Although this is a reference more to ecclesiastical politics than to theology, we can conclude that Lewis's interest in ecumenism was complemented by his immersion into the literary and religious world of one like Richard Hooker and the *via media* of the Anglican divines. In a letter to a frequent correspondent, Don Giovanni Calabria, Lewis writes, "Be assured that for me too schism in the Body of Christ is both a source of grief and a matter for prayers, being a most serious stumbling block to those coming in and one which makes even the faithful weaker in repelling the common foe."[39]

I have found the following statement by Lewis to be the greatest indication of how he considered himself to be influenced by this Anglican divine:

> Every system offers us a model of the universe; Hooker's model has unsurpassed grace and majesty. From much that I have already said it might be inferred that the unconscious tendency of his mind was to secularize. There could be no deeper mistake. Few model universes are more filled — one might say, more drenched — with Deity than his. 'All things that are of God' (and only sin is not) 'have God in them and he them in himself likewise,' yet 'their substance and his wholly differeth' (v. 1 vi. 5). God is unspeakably transcendent; but also unspeakably immanent. It is this conviction which enables Hooker, with no anxiety, to resist any inaccurate claim that is made for revelation against reason, Grace against Nature, the spiritual against the secular.[40]

In the end, Lewis calls Hooker a philosophical genius![41]

Most of the Anglican theologians of the seventeenth century give the impression of a basic unity of thought because of their use of a common theological method: the appeal to reason, Scripture, and antiquity. In fact, we see many of Hooker's ideas worked out to their full conclusions by such seventeenth century divines as Lancelot Andrewes, Jeremy Taylor, and Thomas Traherne, among others. Each of these has developed a theological method which did not, in fact, preclude Marian devotion and reflection because this method is able to find in Mary a locus for the coincidence between the "unspeakably transcendent" and the "unspeakably immanent." Her womb is the "threshold between the material body and the infusion of God's spirit."[42] Peter Kreeft writes about the "co-inherence" of matter with spirit in this way:

> The whole world below was as new as the world above because it was a part of, not apart from, the world above, just as the womb is part of the world. But the fetus does not know this until it is born.
> ... every mother's womb also contained the beginning of something larger than the world, a mind and heart which would contain the whole world. And once a Virgin's womb in one world had contained a God greater than all worlds.[43]

In one like Andrewes, we see a heavy reliance on the methods of expression found in the literature of the Fathers of the Church, and especially the liturgical hymnography of the Greek Fathers.[44] He even goes ahead into the Latin Middle Ages in his references to St. Bernard, for example.[45] He freely makes use of the Marian themes of these Fathers. Using the same method as Hooker, we see that the method of Andrewes encourages a deep appreciation of the role of the Blessed Virgin Mary in the economy of salvation. Lewis read all of these authors and was, by his own admission, impressed by them. In fact, he writes:

> When we look back on the sixteenth century our main impression must be one of narrow escapes and unexpected recoveries. It looked as if our culture was going to be greatly impoverished. Yet somehow the 'upstart' Tudor aristocracy produced a Sidney and became fit to patronize a Spenser, an Inigo Jones, an early Milton. Somehow such an apparent makeshift as the Elizabethan church became the church of Hooker, Donne, Andrewes, Taylor, and Herbert. We stole most of the honey which the humanists were carrying without suffering very much from their stings.[46]

By understanding that the Blessed Virgin Mary had a unique place in traditional Anglican theology, we better appreciate Lewis's own understanding of her place in the economy of salvation, because the one mirrors the other. In fact, three of the divines with whom

Lewis had familiarity — Andrewes, Taylor, and Traherne — are united in their emphasis on the intimacy which God has established with the human person by means of the Incarnation.[47] Humanity thus assumes incomparable value because the Divine Word has assumed the totality of the human condition, excluding, of course, sin. In the foreword to A. M. Allchin's book *The Joy of All Creation*, Edward Yarnold, S. J., writes:

> Canon Allchin sees in the Anglican writers he studies the truths of the Incarnation and the Church coming together in the person of Mary. In all three areas of doctrine (*Sacred Scripture, Tradition, and Magisterium*) there is exemplified the sacramental principle that God comes to his people through the medium of created things. [italics mine][48]

Allchin sees the Anglican divines expressing their mariology more through poetic imagery than through abstract speculation. Their's is an "earthy" mariology, because Mary comes to exemplify what should be the earth's response to the divine initiative. Mary speaks her "yes" at the Annunciation on behalf of all the created world. Her femininity is typical of the original nature of creation's position before the Creator: open, receptive, and obedient. Such a response on the part of nature, Allchin notes according to the divines, is possible since the Fall only because the created world has been sanctified by the Incarnation: "Grace shines through, illuminates and transforms the natural order in its totality, shows that it has a wholly unexpected goal and destiny; for God has entered into the very process of birth."[49] Because of this — the coming together of God and man, flesh and spirit, time and eternity — every human act, which is rooted in nature, "can yet become fully human, in becoming free and consciously realized, can indeed be known as a gift, discovered as a response of thanks to God, can be divine."[50]

By His birth, life, death, and resurrection, the second person of the Holy Trinity has sanctified the whole of creation and guaranteed the sacramental principle that all of creation has the potential for mediating the divine presence in the world. The incarnation has made possible a continuity between the Natural and the Supernatural worlds which was not present before the divine Word assumed the human condition. It seems, indeed, that all of salvation history has been aimed at God's transferral of the Law from stone tablets onto human hearts (Jeremiah 31:33; Ezekiel 36:26) and the divine presence shifting from the Temple to the body of Christ itself (John 2:19-21). This gradual sanctification of all of reality and the move toward greater intimacy between God and His people was certainly a guiding principle in the sacramental theology of the Anglican divines of the seventeenth century, as it undoubtedly formed part of the spiritual heritage which Lewis received and upon which he elaborated his own theology wherein the natural world has the capacity to reflect and contain divine life.

It has been my purpose thus far to introduce the reader to the main themes of Anglican theology in its "Golden Age," especially with regard to those figures who, according to his own admission, were influential in Lewis's thought. Most importantly, we have considered how the seventeenth century Anglican theological emphasis on the centrality of the Incarnation has enabled the Anglican divines of this period to engage in reflection on the place of the Blessed Virgin Mary in the economy of salvation and to develop in their writings and sermons a solid basis for Marian piety and devotion. Studying their particular Marian references would take us too far afield, and this work has already been accomplished, as noted. It is important for us to see C. S. Lewis in the line of this same Anglican tradition — a tradition which finds further expansion in the theology of George Macdonald and Charles Williams.

B. Charles Williams and George Macdonald

Continuing with the first Lewisian thematic of the principle of the Incarnation and the continuity which that principle makes possible between Nature and Super-nature, we note the influence on Lewis's thought of his great friend, Charles Williams. The unity which exists between Creator and the created, between divinity and humanity in Christ finds a particular expression in Williams's writing. Here is what he writes in *The Greater Trumps* describing a church choir singing on Christmas day:

> The mingled voices of men and boys were proclaiming the nature of Christ — 'God and man is one in Christ;' then the boys fell silent, and the men went on, 'One, not by conversion of the Godhead into flesh, but by taking of the manhood into God.' On the assertion they ceased, and the boys rushed joyously in, "One altogether, not" — they looked at the idea and tossed it airily away — '*not* by confusion of substance, but by unity' — they rose, they danced, they triumphed — 'by unity, by unity' — they were silent, all but one, and that one fresh perfection proclaimed the full consummation, each syllable rounded, prolonged, exact — 'by unity of person.'[51]

Charles Hefling, a Williams scholar, concludes from this that

> Williams obviously loved the creed for its crisp precision, among other things. In Christ, Creator and created, deity and humanity, have become one in a definite way, which can be unambiguously stated: 'not by conversion of the Godhead into flesh, but by taking of the manhood into God.' This clause in particular shows up again and again in Williams's prose, and the distinction it draws is no quibble. Should we think of the Incarnation as a contraction of deity, a 'conversion of the Godhead into flesh?' Or was it, as the creed specifies, an intensification of humanity, a 'taking of the manhood into God?'
> ... one of his most original and lasting contributions to Christian thought (was): his theology of romantic love. The fact that the divine Being who is Love itself has become one with the humanity he created means, among other things, that 'any human energy ... is capable of being assumed into sacramental and transcendental heights — such is the teaching of the Incarnation.'[52]

Lewis was greatly influenced by Williams's theology of romantic love — that is, how love between creatures could be sacramental of divine love. In a letter to one of his former students, Dom Bede Griffiths, O.S.B., Lewis writes concerning Williams:

> He is an ugly man with a rather cockney voice. But no one ever thinks of this for 5 (sic) minutes after he has begun speaking. His face becomes almost angelic. Both in public and in private he is of nearly all the men I have met, the one whose address most overflows with *love*. It is simply irresistible. These young men and women were lapping up what he said about Chastity before the end of the hour.[53]

In an effort to make precise the "root principle" of all of Williams's works, Lewis writes:

> [Williams] was a novelist, a poet, a dramatist, a biographer, a critic, and a theologian: a 'romantic theologian' in the technical sense which he himself invented for those words. A romantic theologian does not mean one who is romantic about theology but one who is theological about romance, one who considers the theological implications of those experiences which are called romantic. The belief that the most serious and ecstatic experiences either of human love or of imaginative literature have such theological implications, and that they can be healthy and fruitful only if the implications are diligently thought out and severely lived, is the root principle of all his work.[54]

Of utmost importance in a consideration of Williams's theological contribution to the thought of C. S. Lewis, we may note what Lewis wrote in 1948:

> Two spiritual maxims were constantly present to the mind of Charles Williams: 'This also is Thou' and 'Neither is this Thou.' Holding the first we see that every created thing is, in its degree, an image of God, and the ordinate and faithful appreciation of that thing a clue which, truly followed, will lead back to Him. Holding the second we see that every created thing, the highest devotion to moral duty, the purest conjugal love, the saint and the seraph, is no more than an image, that

> every one of them, followed for its own sake and isolated from its source, becomes an idol whose service is damnation. The first maxim is the formula of the Romantic Way, the 'affirmation of images:' the second is that of the Ascetic Way, the 'rejection of images.' Every soul must in some sense follow both. The Ascetic must honour marriage and poetry and wine and the face of nature even when he rejects them; the Romantic must remember even in his Beatrician moment 'Neither is this Thou.'[55]

In the preceding passage, we notice a certain tension that Lewis (with the help of Williams) is trying to bridge in sacramental theology between the sign and that which is signified by it. Lewis wants to be able to say, along with Hooker and Williams, that "All things that are of God (and only sin is not) have God in them and he them in himself likewise," yet "their substance and his wholly differeth. God is unspeakably transcendent; but also unspeakably immanent." (Ref. endnote #40) It is this type of influence that allows Lewis to construct his theology of the "shadowlands," wherein the shadows somehow participate in that which they image.

Lewis's second major theological theme is the contention that all of reality is hierarchically ordered, from the Supernatural down through the Natural planes. Here we find the influence of the theology of George Macdonald to be particularly strong. We have already said that Lewis's return to the idea of the "Holy," after a long period of atheism, began with the reading of Macdonald's *Phantastes*. Of Macdonald, Lewis writes, "From his own father, he said, he first learned that Fatherhood must be at the core of the universe. He was thus prepared in an unusual way to teach that religion in which the relation of Father and Son is of all relations the most central."[56] Lewis too, as we shall see, is convinced that the hierarchy that exists in the Trinity itself runs through all of created reality.

Lewis learns from Macdonald how allegory and myth — which become the major vehicles for Lewis's own theological expression — are among the best devices for transmitting and defending the essence of the Christian faith. Once again, Lewis writes of Macdonald: "What he does best is fantasy — that hovers between the allegorical and the mythopoeic. And this, in my opinion, he does better than any man."[57]

The third Lewisian thematic receiving tremendous influence from the thought of Charles Williams is the relationship between the Natural and the Supernatural. As has been said earlier, Lewis relates Supernaturalism to Naturalism insofar as he believes that there does exist a level of reality which is distinct from, more important than, and determinative of all other levels while at the same time remaining capable of maintaining a continuity between levels. This we find also to have been a major theme in the writings of Charles Williams. "Natural Goodness" is an essay which Williams published in 1941. It contains all of Williams's main theological themes — those themes which govern all of his books and shorter writings.[58] In it, he writes,

> It is a little unfortunate that in ordinary English talk the words 'natural' and 'supernatural' have come to be considered opposed rather than as complementary. Something like it has happened with those other words 'nature' and 'grace,' but less frequently, since the second two are more often used by trained theologians. But certainly the common use of the first two words implies rather a division between their meanings than a union.
>
> This would be more comprehensible if we meant by 'supernatural' only the world of angels and of God. It is true that God is so wholly 'other' that only in the broadest sense can anything we mean by 'supernatural' be applied to him any more than 'natural.' But of the two terms we must use one rather than the other. And the forces of the world of angels are certainly different from our own 'natural' forces. It is also true that the Christian religion has asserted that those 'natural' forces are but elements, and even infinitesimal elements, in the whole range of creation. But they are so far harmonious with it that they appear contrary only because of that element in man which we call sin, and they are not insignificant or negligible. The 'supernatural' must therefore in some sense include the 'natural.' 'A new earth' was promised as well as 'a new heaven.' Whatever the promise means, that earth is presumably in some relation to this earth.[59]

It is also interesting for our purposes to note a single mariological reference in this same essay:

> ... Even now, in spite of the Athanasian Creed, the single existence of the Incarnate Word is too often almost gnostically contemplated as an inhabitation of the flesh by the Word. But it is not so; what he is, he is wholly and absolutely, and even in his death and in the separation of body and soul he remains wholly and absolutely one. His act could have been to himself alone. He decreed that it should not be; he determined creation; he determined not only to be incarnate, but to be incarnate by means of a mother. He proposed to himself to be born into a world.
>
> This decree upon himself was the decree that brought mankind into being. It was his will to make creatures of such a kind that they should share in that particular joy of his existence in flesh. He bade for himself a mother and all her companions; perhaps the mystery of the mortal maternity of God was greater even than that, but at least it was that. It was the great and single act of active love, consonant with nothing but his nature, compared to which the Redemption (if indeed he were infinitely to maintain all souls alive) was but a sheer act of justice. Our flesh was to hold, to its degree, the secrets of his own.
>
> Nothing has ever altered, nothing could ever alter, that decree. I do not, of course, mean even to seem to separate it from his other acts; only one must speak in terms of time. Certainly he acted altogether, he created and redeemed and judged and executed judgment all at once. But it seems that, as far as we are concerned, he also in that act created process and therefore time, time being in this sense the mere measurement of process. Indeed, so determining to be incarnate by a mother, it might perhaps be said that he determined process for himself also, and even that, for pure increase of joy, he determined that the process should depend on the free will of his mother and of men. He designed exchange of joy; he gave us the final privilege of owing everything to ourselves as well as to him. This moment was our primal nature, and nothing has ever altered that fact — not though we may wish it had.[60]

Indeed how beautiful is this theological reflection of Williams that humankind came into being precisely so that God could be born of a human mother into the human family — that we might participate in this creative joy of his — so great is God's desire for unity with his creation. This is a deeply spiritual way of understanding the essential unity between creation and the Incarnation — between creation and salvation: "all were created through him, and for him. He is before all else that is. In him everything continues in being."[61]

As we have said, "obedience" is a hallmark characteristic of Lewis's theology, and it constitutes the fourth of his major thematics. In this, Lewis thinks once again along the lines of George Macdonald, with whose theology Lewis was completely familiar. In the collection entitled *Unspoken Sermons*, we read in "Abba, Father" the following by Macdonald with regard to "obedience":

> All things were made *through* the Word, but that which was made *in* the Word was life, and that life is the light of men: they who live by this light, that is live as Jesus lived, by obedience, namely, to the Father, have a share in their own making; the light becomes life in them; they are, in their lower way, alive with the life that was first born in Jesus, and through Him has been born in them — by obedience they become one with the Godhead: 'As many as received Him, to them gave he power to become the Sons of God.'[62]

For Macdonald, the "light" of obedience becomes "life" for humankind, and it is by obedience that the human person becomes united to the Trinity. In another sermon Macdonald writes:

> Obedience is the joining of the links of the eternal round. Obedience is but the other side of the creative will. Will is God's will, obedience is man's will; the two make one. The root life, knowing well the thousand troubles it would bring upon Him, has created, and goes on creating, other lives, that though incapable of self-being they may, by willed obedience, share in the bliss of His essential self-ordained being. If we do the will of God, eternal life is ours — no mere continuity of existence, for that in itself is worthless as hell, but a being that is one with the essential life.[63]

Both of the foregoing passages are quoted in Lewis's own anthology of the readings of George Macdonald, where in the Preface Lewis indicates the depth of Macdonald's influence on himself, particularly in regard to the theological thematic of obedience:

> ... And in Macdonald it is always the voice of conscience that speaks. He addresses the will: the demand for obedience, for 'something to be neither more nor less nor other than *done*' is incessant....
> ... I have never concealed the fact that I regarded him as my master; indeed I fancy I have never written a book in which I did not quote from him. But it has not seemed to me that those who have received my books kindly take even now sufficient notice of the affiliation. Honesty drives me to emphasize it. And even if honesty did not — well, I am a don, and 'source-hunting' (*Quellenforschung*) is perhaps in my marrow.[64]

We will see quite clearly in the next chapter how obedience is also at the heart of the theology of C. S. Lewis.

Lastly, we find the typical Lewisian thematic of the ordering of all reality — Supernatural and Natural — along the lines of the masculine-feminine relationship deep-rooted once again in the works of Lewis's close friend, Charles Williams. As mentioned above, Williams's theology of romantic love is "one of his most original and lasting contributions to Christian thought."[65] This theology teaches that the incarnation of divine love occurs most often in the human experience of the lover's relationship with the beloved. Williams says that he has taken much of this theology from Dante, because he is "the greatest European poet ... and because no one else has given us so complete an exposition of the Way of Romantic Love."[66] Surely Lewis, too, held Dante in the highest esteem, as is evidenced by his own masterful literary and theological critique entitled *Preface to Paradise Lost*.[67] We see Williams's theology of romantic love to be at the heart of the *The Allegory of Love* and *Perelandra*, two masterworks of the fiction of C. S. Lewis.

The theological heritage and influence on the thought of C. S. Lewis by classical seventeenth century Anglican theology and by the theology of more contemporary authors and friends like George

Macdonald and Charles Williams sets the stage for the development of Lewis's major theological thematics, as have been outlined in this chapter. We now turn to a detailed consideration of the second book of Lewis's "space trilogy," *Perelandra*, wherein we find all of these thematics at work and at the heart of which Lewis situates a figure who may be referred to as a "new Eve."

---

1. C. S. Lewis, *Mere Christianity*, cf. "Preface," especially p. viii, where Lewis says, in part, referring to the Church, "It is at her centre, where her truest children dwell, that each communion is really closest to every other in spirit, if not in doctrine. And this suggests that at the centre of each there is something, or a Someone, who against all divergences of belief, all differences of temperament, all memories of mutual persecution, speaks with the same voice."

2. cf. Chapter XIV ("The Grand Miracle") of Lewis's 1947 book entitled *Miracles*.

3. Ibid., pp. 46-7.

4. Ibid., pp. 143-55

5. C. S. Lewis, *Surprised by Joy* — The Shape of My Early Life. (New York: Inspirational Press, 1994), pp. 19-20.

6. Allchin, *The Joy of All Creation*, An Anglican Meditation on the Place of Mary. (Cambridge, MA: Cowley Publications, 1984), p. 9.

7. George Macdonald, *Phastastes, A Faerie Romance*. (London: J. M. Dent and Sons Ltd.).

8. C. S. Lewis, *Surprised by Joy*, p. 99.

9. C. S. Lewis, *Letters of C. S. Lewis*, Edited, with a Memoir, by W. H. Lewis. (New York: Harcourt, Brace & World, Inc., 1966), p. 176.

10. F. L. Cross & E. A. Livingstone, eds., *The Oxford Dictionary of the Christian Church*. (Oxford: Oxford University Press, 1983), p. 1487.

11. C. S. Lewis, *Letters*, p. 206.

12. Ibid., p. 177.

13. Ibid.

14. C. S. Lewis, *Surprised by Joy*, p. 123.

15. Ibid., p. 118.

16. A. M. Allchin, "Preface" to George Herbert, *The Country Parson* and *The Temple* in *The Classics of Western Spirituality*, John N. Wall, Jr., ed. (New York: Paulist Press, 1981), p. xii.

17. Ibid., p. xv.

18. C. S. Lewis, *Surprised by Joy*, p. 118.

19. C. S. Lewis, *English Literature in the Sixteenth Century Excluding Drama*. (Oxford: Clarendon Press, 1954), p. 319.

20. Julian Davies, *The Caroline Captivity of the Church*, Charles I and the Remoulding of Anglicanism, 1625-1641. (Oxford: Clarendon Press, 1992).

Nicholas Lossky, *Lancelot Andrewes the Preacher (1555-1626)*, The Origins of the Mystical Theology of the Church of England. (Oxford: Clarendon Press, 1991).

Henry R. McAdoo, *The Spirit of Anglicanism*, A Survey of Anglican Theological Method in the Seventeenth Century. (New York: Charles Scribner's Sons, 1965).

Stephen Neill, *Anglicanism*. (Oxford: Mowbrays, 1997).

Aidan Nichols, O.P., *The Panther and the Hind*, A Theological History of Anglicanism. (Edinburgh: T and T Clark, 1993).

John William Packer, *The Transformation of Anglicanism 1643-1660*. (Manchester: University of Manchester Press, 1969).

Carroll E. Simcox, *The Historical Road of Angelicanism*. (Chicago: Henry Regnery Company, 1968).

Jeremy Taylor, *Jeremy Taylor, Selected Works*. Thomas K. Carroll, ed. in *The Classics of Western Spirituality*. (Mahwah, N. J.: Paulist Press, 1990).

Nicholas Tyacke, *Anti-Calvinists*, The Rise of English Arminianism c. 1590-1640. (Oxford: Clarendon Press, 1987).

21. Lucien Richard, *Christ the Self-Emptying of God*. (New York: Paulist Press, 1997), pp. 196-97.

22. Ibid., p. 197.

23. C. S. Lewis, *English Literature*, pp. 451-63.

24. Roger Lancelyn Green and Walter Hooper, *C. S. Lewis, A Biography*. (New York: Harcourt Brace Jovanovich, 1974), p. 116.

25. Allchin in *The Classics of Western Spirituality*, p. xiv.

26. cf. *Surprised by Joy* and *Letters of C. S. Lewis*.

27. George Herbert, *The Temple* in *The Classics of Western Spirituality*, John N. Wall, Jr., ed. (New York: Paulist Press, 1981), pp. 195-6.

28. op. cit.

29. variously published from 1593-1666.

30. "Hooker, Richard" in *The Oxford Dictionary of the Christian Church*, F. L. Cross and E. A. Livingstone, eds. (Oxford: Oxford University Press, 1983), p. 665.

31. Lewis, *English Literature*, p. 451.

32. From Hooker's sermon "Of Justification" quoted in Lewis, *English Literature*, ibid.

33. Lewis, *English Literature*, ibid., p. 453.

34. Ibid., p. 454.

35. McAdoo, *The Spirit of Anglicanism*, ibid., p. 6.

36. C. S. Lewis, *The Abolition of Man*. (New York: Macmillan Publishing Company, 1947), p. 29.

37. Lewis, *English Literature*, pp. 453-4.

38. Ibid., p. 454.

39. C. S. Lewis, *Letters — C. S. Lewis — Don Giovanni Calabria — A Study in Friendship*, Martin Moynihan, ed. (London: Collins, 1989), p. 31.

40. Lewis, *English Literature*, ibid., pp. 459-60.

41. Ibid., p. 463.

42. Allchin, *The Joy of All Creation*, ibid., cover page commentary.

43. Peter Kreeft, *Heaven — The Heart's Deepest Longing*. (San Francisco: Ignatius Press, 1989), pp. 280-81.

44. Allchin, *The Joy of All Creation*, ibid., pp. 19-20.

45. Ibid., p. 21.

46. Lewis, *English Literature*, pp. 557-8.

47. Edward Yarnold, S. J., "Foreword" in Allchin, *The Joy of All Creation*, ibid., pp. ix-x.

48. Ibid., p. ix. N.b. It would be beyond the purview of this present study of C. S. Lewis to examine the mariological references of these seventeenth century authors. The reader is referred to Allchin's extensive study of these themes in the work cited above.

49. Allchin, *The Joy of All Creation*, ibid., p. 4.

50. Ibid.

51. Charles Williams, *The Greater Trumps*. (New York: Pellegrini and Cudahay, 1950), p. 125.

52. Charles Hefling, ed., *Charles Williams: Essential Writings in Spirituality and Theology*. (Cambridge, MA: Cowley Publications, 1993), pp. 9-12.

53. C. S. Lewis, *Letters*, pp. 196-7.

54. C. S. Lewis et. al., *Essays Presented to Charles Williams*. (Grand Rapids, MI: Eerdmans, 1966), p. vi.

55. C. S. Lewis in Charles Williams's *Taliessin Through Logres, The Region of the Summer Stars, Arthurian Torso*. (Grand Rapids, MI: Eerdmans, 1974), p. 335.

56. C. S. Lewis, *George Macdonald: An Anthology*. Edited and with a preface by C. S. Lewis. (New York: Simon and Schuster, 1996), p. xxi.

57. Ibid., p. xxvi.

58. Charles Hefling in *Charles Williams*, ibid., p. 7.

59. Charles Williams, "Natural Goodness" in Hefling, ed., *Charles Williams: Essential Writings*, ibid., pp. 35-6.

60. Ibid., pp. 36-7.

61. Colossians 1:16b-17.

62. George Macdonald, *An Anthology*. Edited and with a preface by C. S. Lewis. (New York: Simon and Schuster, 1996), p. 55.

63. Ibid., p. 61.

64. C. S. Lewis, *George Macdonald: An Anthology*, ibid., pp. xxx-xxxii.

65. Charles Hefling in *Charles Williams*, ibid., p. 11-12.

66. Charles Williams, "The Theology of Romantic Love" in *Charles Williams: Essential Writings*, Charles Hefling, ed., ibid., pp. 84-85.

67. C. S. Lewis, *A Preface* to *Paradise Lost*. (London: Oxford University Press, 1942).

Chapter Three
The Marian Attitude In Christian Theology

C. S. Lewis has not developed a mariology, per se, in his writings. This fact, however, does not preclude appreciating in his work the development of what he thinks to be the proper attitude of the individual Christian before God. His major theological themes, and his references — however minimal — to the person of the Blessed Virgin Mary and her place in the mystery of salvation, allow us to state categorically that Lewis advocated a "Marian attitude" as the proper Christian attitude toward God. We find this to be especially true in the second book of his "space trilogy" entitled *Perelandra*, in particular with reference to the figure of the female character, Tinidril.

In order to present what I consider to be Lewis's "Marian attitude" as the proper Christian attitude in general, it is first necessary to establish accepted parameters for a definition of Christian holiness, for it is by "holiness" that Christian persons are situated in their relationship to the Divine. What type of attitude, for Lewis, characterizes the person who is considered "holy" in the sight of God and all? Generally speaking, spiritual theologians would consider "mysticism" to be a category — perhaps the most intense category — of Christian holiness. One can be holy without being a mystic, but it is the perfection of mysticism towards which all holiness naturally tends. We can deduce, therefore, the proper Christian attitude which characterizes holiness by a consideration of mysticism — that which is considered to be a perfection of holiness. "Mysticism" may be defined as "A special, deep experience of union with and knowledge of the divine reality, freely granted by God."[1] Now union with and knowledge of divine reality is never quantifiable in a person's life. The mystic's closeness to God and knowledge of God, of its very nature (that is, mystical!), can be fully communicated neither through the spoken or the written word. Christian mysticism is made possible by the human person's experience of the Word made flesh in Jesus Christ. The Christian's experiences of the living Christ constitute that person's relationship to Christ. But not every "relationship" with God in Christ is "mystical" because divine intimacy and knowledge are gifts freely granted by the Creator to whomever He wills, and the towering heights of mysticism have only been attributed to a few throughout history. If mysticism resides in the towering heights of Christian holiness, and if union with and knowledge of the divine reality is constitutive of mysticism, then the category of "union" with the divine must also in some sense characterize all levels of Christian holiness.

C. S. Lewis wrote about union with God in a way that captured the imagination of his readers. Much of his fiction has mystical overtones. He was aware of the fact that this sense of mystical union is only approached through the door of contemplation. One of Lewis's popular works is the complex allegory *The Pilgrim's Regress*, in which he tells the story of a dream he once had of a boy named John who undertakes a life-long and world-wide journey in search of enlightenment and fulfillment, finding at the end of his journey that these things are granted to the pilgrim by someone — in the story, the "Landlord" — the allegorical figure for God. John is led across the final canyon which separates him from the Landlord's Castle by the "Lady" named "Contemplation." Lewis takes pains to describe, allegorically, the nature of this mystical union into which John is initiated by Contemplation as being not a "jump" into some kind of impersonal, all-pervasive, pantheistic reality into which one escapes in order to save oneself from the world, but a deliberate "dive" down to the very depths of the waters of death so as to rise up again through a tunnel, the entrance to which is far beneath the surface of the water. A "dive" would bring one further down into the water than would a "jump." As the character "Mother Kirk" ("Mother Church") tells John: "If you jump, you will be trying to save yourself and you may be hurt. As well, you would not go deep enough."[2] Lewis's use of this allegorical language reflects his own life's experiences during his journey to faith. A string of intellectual "jumps" landed him into such varied philosophies and ways of life as enlightened selfishness, psychologism, pragmatism, humanism, pantheism, absolutism. John learns from Mother Kirk that there is a particular way for him to dive into the life-giving waters — the way which Lewis himself found in his own life to be uniquely "in Christ." Like Christ, John must dive into death to self in order to rise again to the life of God. Doing so, he will rise to that vision of beauty which he has been seeking all his life (the longed-for "Island" of his life's visions). He had been taught throughout his childhood that the "Landlord" was in control of the destiny of all people and arriving at the Landlord's Castle was the fulfillment of that destiny. The Landlord's Castle can thus be seen as one with — the same as — the Island, as well as the longed-for "Eastern mountains."

John is told that the way to this paradise is back through the world. Thus he is sent not directly to the Island or to the Landlord's Castle, but back where he came from (hence the title *The Pilgrim's Regress*) where with renewed vision he will see that behind all of created reality there exist vast realms of Divine reality. In this way, Lewis achieves the aim of all of his apologetical fiction: to baptize the human imagination or to sensitize the human mind to the ultimate realities which lie behind the world of nature and which the world of nature reflects. In this way also we can understand the sacramental relationship which Lewis perceives to exist in nature's reflection of Supernature. In fact, we might call this relationship between nature and Supernature a Marian kind of relationship — with nature being the womb, as it were, of Supernature as Mary provided her womb for the incarnate Word, even as the Church had its birthing from Israel and, for us, immortal life (*zoe*) resides in and springs forth from natural life (*bios*).

The Mystery Of Our Union With God In Christ Via The "Marian Attitude"

In order to achieve union with God (which is the fundamental principle of Christian holiness) Lewis would maintain that we need to recognize and accept the sacramentality of nature, because only then can we recognize and respond to God's Word as it expresses itself in and through our experience in the world — just as Mary recognized the Divine initiative taken at the Annunciation and responded positively to it. Hence for Lewis, as for the seventeenth-century Anglican divines, all reality (except sin) is recognized as having sacramental value. The Marian attitude recognizes the sacramental value of all reality. Let us attempt to elaborate on the meaning and significance of that attitude.

According to the "Dogmatic Constitution on the Church" — *Lumen Gentium* — of the Second Vatican Council, the Church exists "in the nature of sacrament — a sign and instrument, that is, of communion with God and of unity among all men ..."[3] The Church exists for the purpose of bringing humankind into communion with God. Christian holiness, indeed, is constituted by union with God and all people are called to this holiness, each "according to his own gifts and duties."[4] Since each Christian advances along the way of faith to holiness according to his particular state in life, we must undertake an examination of the various types of union into which God invites every human person and the nature of the attitude which properly responds to this invitation. Having the Marian attitude in response to God's call to communion with Himself is the proper form of response of human persons to the various types of union into which God invites them.

Within the context of the various types of union into which God calls His people according to their state in life (e.g., priestly, religious, laity), the Second Vatican Council makes it clear that there is an essential unity to Christian holiness. A very important line in the fifth chapter of *Lumen Gentium*, which went through a number of revisions before the final draft was accepted, reads as follows: "The forms and tasks of life are many but holiness is one ..."[5] There is an essential unity underlying all types of Christian holiness and this unity is most clearly perceived in an understanding of the Marian attitude, which is the quintessentially Christian attitude.

Mary herself was called to a variety of types of union with God, each of which she responded to positively by her *fiat*. We may here indicate four of these types of union: incarnational, mystical, communicative, and associative. Mary is called to incarnational union with God in virtue of her motherhood. She gives flesh to the God-man and is rightly called *theotokos* — God-bearer.[6] Her union with God is mystical in virtue of her spiritual marriage and union with the Logos. Her union with God is also communicative in that she is the prayerful one, pondering the Word in her heart from the Annunciation and the infancy through the childhood of Jesus, and then being prayerfully present with the Apostles at the coming of the Holy Spirit on the first Pentecost.[7] Finally, she enjoys an associative union with the Lord as His associate and handmaid in the work of redemption.[8] M. J. Scheeben points out that St. Thomas attributes the privileges associated with divine motherhood to three categories of her union with the Godhead:

> 1) The relation of the mother to the child, or to the Son as her bodily fruit, in so far as the mother must be honored by the Son and the honor of the latter was conditioned by that of the mother;
> 2) Mary's affinity to Christ, whereby she was united with Him as with her spiritual head;
> 3) Mary's relation to the Godhead, dwelling bodily within her, whereby she is united with the Godhead in a manner analogous to that of the body with the spirit.[9]

All of these categories of union are realized within the context of a personal relationship between the Blessed Virgin Mary and God. The relationship is made possible by God's grace and Mary's faith in God's plan for the salvation of herself and all humankind.

1. The Early Church's Search For A Marian Attitude

The early Fathers of the Church were themselves more interested in Mary's faith and in her place in God's plan for salvation than in any of the personal privileges which later developed as objects of Marian devotion. In fact, what concerned the early Fathers most of all is that which brings unity to the many-faceted Marian vocation: Mary's attitude. The second century apologists like Ignatius of Antioch, Justin, Irenaeus, and Tertullian believed that the mystery of the whole divine economy of salvation was both enclosed and expressed in the life of Mary.[10] This is especially true inasmuch as the early Fathers saw Mary as the "Second Eve." Beginning with Justin (d. ca. 165) — a Greek philosopher and apologist — we find the roots of the Eve — Mary parallel to be part of an ancient tradition in the Church, close to the Apostolic tradition and developed with at least implicit reference to Sacred Scripture.

In the first book of his *Apologies Against the Gentiles*,[11] Justin writes that Jesus Christ is the unique and first-born Son of the Father. By God's power, He was born of the Virgin, in fulfillment of the Old Testament prophecies. Justin argues that the Virgin Birth is not a product of Greek mythology but a truly miraculous event. Now this miraculous birth is accomplished by God for purposes of reversing the activity of the serpent who brings to bear his evil plan in Eve. God therefore has a plan (economy) to confront the devil's "economy." Thus do we see the first development in Christian history of this theology of reversal of economies which is the foundation for the theological thematic of the Eve — Mary parallel. This becomes even more explicit in two passages of Justin's *Dialogue with the Jew Trypho*:

> ... this Christ, Son of God, who was before the morning star and the moon, and submitted to become incarnate, and be born of this virgin of the family of David, in order that, by this dispensation, the serpent that sinned from the beginning, and the angels like him, may be destroyed, and that death may be condemned ...[12]

and

> For Eve, who was a virgin and undefiled, having conceived the word of the serpent, brought forth disobedience and death. But the Virgin Mary received faith and joy, when the angel Gabriel announced the good tidings ... and she replied 'Be it done unto me according to thy word.'[13]

It is in this text that Mary is opposed to Eve for the first time in ancient Christian literature. For Justin, Eve's disobedience "conceived the word of the serpent" and brought forth death, while Mary's obedience to God's Word brought forth faith, joy, and Life. Therefore, the salvation of humankind was accomplished, according to Justin, in the line of obedience. Obedience is fundamental to the Marian attitude.

Justin's argumentation in defense of Mary's divine maternity and virginity is essentially that of an apologist-philosopher whose primary purpose was to defend the divine economy before pagans and Jews. These attributes of Mary become themselves the roots or foundation of what will later become a theological thematic of the Eve — Mary parallel. Both Mary and Eve were to be considered, each in their own turn, as mother of all the living. Only in light, then, of their soteriological function do divine motherhood and virginity come to be viewed as "prerogatives" of Mary. Mary's "oneness" with God in her obedient acceptance of His saving plan makes her who she is — at once virgin and mother. In God's plan ontology follows soteriology.

While Justin may have planted the seed of the Eve — Mary parallel, reference to Mary as "New Eve" or "Second Eve" was to come later on. These terms became more suggested or implicit in the Christian writers shortly after Justin, like Irenaeus of Lyon (b. ca. 140-146) in the Eastern tradition and Tertullian (b. ca. 155) in the Western tradition. The point is that as early as the second century in Christian tradition, Mary's "obedience" (in opposition to the disobedience of Eve) has been understood as a central element in Mary's attitude towards God's plan for salvation. Equally as important is the bridge which subsequent Fathers begin to make between Mary and the Church. Hence, from early Christian times, Mary has been seen as representative of the mystery of salvation. To examine, therefore, the individual mysteries of Mary one by one (Mother, Bride, Prayerful One, Associate) is not enough to appreciate the depth and fullness of the Marian attitude. We need one basic principle or attribute which will unify all other Marian images and penetrate deeply into the mystery of salvation. In an attempt to place Mariology on an equal level with Ecclesiology as doctrinal or dogmatic tracts within the scope of theological study, Otto Semmelroth notes how the early Church Fathers searched for a basic principle which would equate the figure of Mary and the Church. They found this basic principle, attribute, or "attitude" to have been established in Mary by God, and they charged theology with the task of representing this attitude to the Church. Semmelroth writes:

> The divine idea that vivifies Mary and totally governs her concrete existence must show her to us as the figure standing, in her role as Mediator, between Christ and grace. The Church must be similarly considered. It is immediately clear that the divine idea is realized in the Church and that the Church functions for man's redemption according to the pattern of this idea. With this comparison made, it may possibly be proved that the idea underlying both the concept of Mary and the concept of the Church is the same.[14]

Central to this "idea" which unites Mary and the Church is the "Marian attitude":

> We will have to order our lives (received somehow in the Church through Mary) according to the life led by the Archetype before us ... It is Mary's *attitude* that established her as an example for the Christian, and her *attitude* flows from her being rooted in God, a fact she expressed to the Angel at the Annunciation: 'Behold the handmaid of the Lord' ... From this she drew the conclusion that was to mark her entire life: 'Be it done unto me according to Thy Word.'[15] (emphasis mine)

From the time of the earliest Church Fathers, with their attempts to arrive at an understanding of the innermost reality of Mary, the Church has sought to locate in Mary the key to its own innermost nature. A return to the most ancient traditions has shown that, with Mary as its archetype,

> The essential task of the Church ... is to assume Christ's work as His Bride and thereby to participate in its fruits.
> ... The Church is the Bride of Christ because of the *fiat* she pronounces to her Bridegroom's work; receiving His fruits she is joined to Him in the mystical-physical oneness of His Mystical Body ...
> ... Mary, that is to say the Church, has become 'disposed' for the reception of the Arch-Sacrament, the Incarnate God and His sacrifice on the Cross. Because of this *receptivity*, or rather through it, 'the fullness of blessings has been deposited in her.'[16] (emphasis mine)

Mary is the archetype of the Church in her *fiat* which grounds her own and the Church's divine motherhood, spousal quality, and associativeness in the work of redemption. The obedience of Mary is most essential to the Marian attitude, along with the quality of receptivity to the Incarnate God. Obedience and receptivity become for the Church a *pleroma* (or a fullness of blessings) which enable the Church to accomplish its task of establishing communion with God and unity among all people.

2. A Marian Attitude In Recent Magisterial Documents

The Church's appreciation of the person of the Blessed Mary and the role she plays in God's economy of salvation has matured throughout history and finds exquisite expression especially in the mariology which has been developed in the Church since the Second Vatican Council. Indeed, it will be my intention to show how the major themes of Lewisian theology as described in Chapter One find resonance in five recent magisterial documents with particular Marian content. These documents are: Chapter VIII of the Dogmatic Constitution on the Church *Lumen Gentium*, the Apostolic

Exhortation *Marialis Cultus* of Pope Paul VI, the Encyclical *Redemptoris Mater* and the Apostolic Letter *Mulieris Dignitatem* of Pope John Paul II, and the new *Catechism of the Catholic Church*.

Let us remind ourselves of Lewis's five major themes before we hear their resonance in recent magisterial pronouncements concerning the Blessed Virgin Mary. Those themes are: the centrality of the Incarnation in the economy of salvation, the hierarchical ordering of all reality, the discontinuity and continuity between Supernaturalism and Naturalism, obedience, and the relation of the masculine to the feminine aspects of reality according to the Supernatural archetype of this relationship.

a. *Lumen Gentium* VIII: Of The Blessed Virgin, Mother Of God In The Mystery Of Christ And Of The Church.

The history of the development of the eighth chapter of *Lumen Gentium* is a somewhat complex history. It was complicated from the start when — on October 29, 1963 — the first Mariological vote of the Fathers of Vatican II went in favor of placing a schema on the Blessed Virgin Mary as a chapter within the Constitution on the Church. The importance of the placement of this document lay in the tension that existed in Catholic theology between what may be called "Christotypism" and "ecclesiotypism."[17] "Christoptypism" would have found expression in the ideas of those who wished to situate the Blessed Virgin Mary between Christ and the Church as somehow below the rank of the former but above the rank of the latter. "Ecclesiotypism" would rather situate Mary within the context of the Church, she being the type (*typus*) of the Church in its relationship to Christ. It would seem that the decision to place a consideration of Mary as a chapter within the Constitution on the Church constituted a yielding to the ecclesiotypical perspective. Nonetheless, the very title of the chapter makes clear the desire of the Council Fathers to present Mary in her unique relationship to Christ as willed by God in the economy of salvation. This would safeguard the emphasis of the Christotypical perspective.[18] Thus, while the chapter does not consider Marian "privileges," it does consider what the Fathers believed to be essential in Catholic mariology — Mary's role in the plan of God.

i. Introduction — LG #s 52-54

The opening paragraph (#52) begins with the citation of Galatians 4:4, which points out that God in His goodness effected the redemption of the world "when the fullness of time came, God sent his son, born of a woman ..." The document thus begins by placing Mary at the heart of the history of salvation, by identifying this woman as the human instrument God selected to bring about the Incarnation of the second person of the Trinity. This beginning is in direct accord with the first of Lewis's five major themes, namely, the centrality of the Incarnation in the economy of salvation. It is only in relation to the saving event of the Incarnation that Mary "is acknowledged and honored as being truly the Mother of God and of the redeemer" (#53). Her "high office and dignity" proceed directly from her intimate union "by a close and indissoluble tie" with her Son. Hence what is most essential about Mary is that she is *"theotokos"* — God-bearer. Paragraph number 52 goes on to recognize Mary's place as far surpassing all creatures because of the sublime grace of intimacy which she shares with her Son, an intimacy which enabled her to join in charity "in bringing about the birth of believers in the Church, who are members of its head." In this she is the Church's "type and outstanding model in faith and charity." At the same time, she is recognized as being fully human, "united to all those who are to be saved."

Again, paragraph number 54 reiterates the Council Fathers' intention that Mary is to be essentially considered in her role "in the mystery of the Incarnate Word and the Mystical Body." And finally, at the end of this introductory section of the eighth chapter of *Lumen Gentium*, the Fathers make it clear that they do not "intend to give a complete doctrine on Mary, nor ... to decide those questions which the work of theologians has not yet fully clarified" (#54). The Council only wants to consider that which is most essential — the centrality of the Incarnation in the economy of salvation and the role of the Blessed Virgin Mary in that economy.

ii. LG #s 55-59: The Function Of The Blessed Virgin In The Plan Of Salvation

The whole thrust of the next section of *Lumen Gentium* is to situate Mary's function in the plan of salvation in relation to Christ and the Church. Once again, Mary is presented here as privileged only with relation to her place in God's saving plan. Paragraph #55 points out that this is shown throughout the sacred writings of the Old and New Testament as well as in the Church's tradition. It is only as "Mother of the Redeemer" that her figure is brought into "clearer light" (#55). The Incarnation is central, not the Marian privileges. The Incarnation is the central saving work of God and the time of salvation is fulfilled in "the exalted Daughter of Zion" (#55). Obedience, humility, and receptivity to the word and will of God — all Lewisian themes — find expression in this paragraph in the sentence: "She stands out among the poor and humble of the Lord, who confidently hope for and receive salvation from him" (#55).

Paragraph #56 attempts to shed light on the "entirely unique holiness" of the Blessed Virgin Mary — she who was hailed as "full of grace" by the Angel Gabriel at the Annunciation. Again, her unique status in the Communion of Saints hails from the fact of her predestination by God to assent freely to the Incarnation — "so that just as a woman had a share in bringing about death, so also should a woman contribute to life" (#56). Mary is that woman whose obedience at the Annunciation counteracts the disobedience of Eve in the Garden of Eden. Such a predestination grounds Mary's complete preservation from sin (she is the Immaculate Conception) and paves the way for "an entirely unique holiness" (#56).

The theme of Mary's obedience and the totality of her self-giving to the saving plan of God resounds throughout this paragraph as an active rather than a passive receptivity on her part to God's work: "the Fathers see Mary not merely as passively engaged by God, but as freely cooperating in the work of man's salvation through faith and obedience" (#56).

Christian holiness as intimate union with Christ is elaborated upon in paragraph 57, where "this union of the mother with the Son" is illustrated throughout Christ's earthly life by Gospel references to Mary's involvement in the saving events of her Son's life (the Visitation, the Virgin Birth, the visit of the shepherds and the magi, the Presentation of Jesus in the Temple, and the finding of Jesus in the temple). This same theme of Mary's involvement in the saving deeds of her Son's public life continues in paragraph

58. Reference is made to her presence at Cana (John 2:1-11), her Son's declaration of her blessedness because of her attention to the word of God (Mark 3:35 and Luke 11:27), and her faithful perseverance "in union with her Son unto the cross." On Calvary, she was uniquely one with Christ's sufferings and she "associated herself with his sacrifice in her mother's heart ... lovingly consenting to the immolation of this victim which was born of her" (#58). This constitutes a clear illustration of the nature of Christian holiness as it is presented in the theology of C. S. Lewis — that is, holiness as union with Christ. We have seen how it is in the Marian attitude that all types of union with God (incarnational, associative, communicative and mystical) find common ground. Obedience and receptivity to the word of God are major characteristics of the Marian attitude as it is presented in the works of Lewis and in this section of Chapter VIII of *Lumen Gentium*.

The final paragraph (#59) of this second section of LG VIII sheds light on the Blessed Virgin's communicative or prayerful union not only with her Son, but also with her Son's body — the Church. This is done by reference to Mary's presence with the Apostles in the Upper Room at Pentecost (Acts 1:14). And finally, her mystical union with Christ is attested to in this paragraph with reference to her glorious Assumption and exaltation as Queen of all things, "that she might be the more fully conformed to her Son" (#59). In LG 55-59, the Council Fathers have given us a picture of the holiness of Mary in terms of a category of union. This category of union with God in Christ is supported by two central Lewisian themes: the centrality of the Incarnation in the economy of salvation and the thematic of obedience. Mary's union with God in Christ is owing to her role in the Incarnation — a role characterized by obedience, openness and receptivity to the word of God. Her divine motherhood and her spiritual maternity of all the redeemed is the direct result of her association with the Incarnation — her cooperation "by her obedience, faith, hope, and burning charity in the work of the Savior" (#61).

Let us move on now to another magisterial document which also resonates with the central themes of Lewisian theology.

b. *Marialis Cultus*

It must be admitted that C. S. Lewis is lacking in his expression of Marian devotion. This is, of course, due to the Protestant theological heritage to which he was an heir. This is an important fact to take into consideration when judging the value of Lewis's contribution to mariology, since the document we are now considering, *Marialis Cultus* (1974) of Pope Paul VI, makes the point that sacred worship and devotion is the primary task of the People of God (MC, intro.). Certainly, Lewis neither venerates nor advocates veneration to the Blessed Virgin Mary in his written works. This shortcoming could be seen to compromise Lewis's understanding of the place of Mary in the mystery of Christ as that understanding has been developed in Catholic theology. But, as has been noted above, Lewis did not even consider himself a theologian, hence we cannot expect to find a developed mariology in his work! While respect for the plan of God implies veneration of Mary (MC, intro.), it can be said that Lewis held Mary in great esteem for the role which she played in God's saving work at least during her earthly sojourn.

Although *Marialis Cultus* is a document which is mainly concerned with the place of Mary in Christian worship, we do find in it many parallels with some of Lewis's central theological themes and with the "Marian attitude" as that attitude has been defined in this present work. Consider the centrality of the Incarnation in the economy of salvation (or the "Grand Miracle," as Lewis called it). Pope Paul VI clearly states that "In the Virgin Mary, everything is relative to Christ and dependent on him" (MC 24). The idea that any devotion to the Blessed Virgin should have Christ as its point of reference (MC 4) would be accommodated by Lewis's theology of the centrality of the Incarnation. In fact, Mary's "singular dignity" is wrought only in the context of the mystery of Christ's birth. She is that "holy mother ... through whom we were found worthy to receive the Author of life" (MC 5). The Pope refers to Mary's joy as the result of her dialogue with God and her "active and responsible consent" to an "event of world importance" (MC 37).

Obedience is another Lewisian thematic which finds resonance in *Marialis Cultus*. The solemnity of the Annunciation in part commemorates the obedience and faithfulness of the Blessed Virgin Mary, the New Eve, "who with her generous 'fiat' (cf. Luke 1:18) became, through the working of the Spirit, the Mother of God" (MC 6). Also, this document refers to Mary as "the attentive Virgin, who receives the Word of God with faith" (MC 17); she is also called "the Virgin in prayer" (MC 18). The *Magnificat* is her prayer *par excellance* "in which there mingles the joy of the ancient and new Israel" (MC 18). She is become the Virgin mother because "believing and obeying ... (she) ... brought forth on earth the Father's Son" (MC 18). In her obedience to the Father's will, she provides the faithful with a "lesson and example ... (of) ... the way and means of one's own sanctification" (MC 21).

Another of Lewis's central themes is that all of reality is hierarchically ordered — a hierarchy patterned after the relationships among the members of the three-personed Trinity. *Marialis Cultus* refers to the Feast of the Lord's Presentation in the Temple as showing "the continuity of the fundamental offering that the Incarnate Word made to the Father when he entered the world" (MC 20). For Lewis, such kenosis characterizes the activity of each member of the Trinity for all time — before and after the Incarnation. In this, the Church sees the "universal nature of salvation" to be one of offering, in terms of Lewis's major themes, of the Son to the Father in the life of the Trinity — an offering characterized by obedience in an hierarchically-ordered reality. Mary's offering of Jesus in the Temple thus mirrors the universal nature of salvation which "reaches its climax on Calvary" (MC 20) for both Son and mother, who " 'lovingly consented to the immolation of this victim which she herself had brought forth' and also was offering to the Eternal Father" (MC 20).

A fourth Lewisian theme echoed in *Marialis Cultus* is that of masculine and feminine archetypes and the relationship of man and woman to each other in marriage. For Lewis, the danger inherent in the marriage relationship in a fallen world (e.g., domination of one partner over another) can only be avoided when the archetypical realities of gender are regarded as the model for imitation. *Marialis Cultus* tells us that the Fathers of the Church "saw in the mysterious relationship between the Spirit and Mary as aspect redolent of marriage" (MC 26). In becoming the spouse of the Holy Spirit, Mary received from the Spirit as from God the Father a fullness of grace and an abundance of faith, hope and charity, which altogether provided her with "the strength that sustained her acceptance of the will of God, and the vigour that upheld her in her suffering at the foot of the cross" (MC 26). The Spirit of Christ, who is the Spouse of the Church, and its feminine complement, which we find in Mary, represent the archetypical realities of masculine and feminine which characterize not only the proper relationship between the sexes, but the even more important relationship between God and humanity as a whole.

Because so many of Lewis's central themes are present (implicitly or overtly) in *Marialis Cultus*, we should not be surprised that the Marian attitude which this magisterial document presents is strikingly similar to the Marian attitude that we have found throughout the works of the author being studied. The Pope writes:

> Mary (is) a model of the spiritual attitude with which the Church celebrates and lives the divine mysteries ... the Blessed Virgin is ... a most excellent exemplar of the Church in the order of faith, charity, and perfect union with Christ, that is, of the interior disposition with which the Church, the beloved spouse, closely associated with her Lord, invokes Christ and through him worships the eternal Father (MC 16).

Since *Marialis Cultus* deals mainly with the celebration of the sacred mysteries and the honor that is due the Blessed Virgin Mary in the context of those mysteries, it follows that the Church should assume an attitude that is similar to that of the Virgin (MC 23). This "Marian attitude" is an indispensable characteristic of the Christian life, for the Church defines itself by the way in which it prays (*lex orandi, lex credendi*). Interestingly enough, Pope Paul VI adds, "Catholics are also united with Anglicans, whose classical theologians have already drawn attention to the sound scriptural basis for devotion to the Mother of Our Lord, while those of the present day increasingly underline the importance of Mary's place in the Christian life" (MC 32).

c. *Redemptoris Mater*

Pope John Paul II decided from the very beginning of his pontificate to place his entire future ministry under Mary's maternal care (as evidenced by his Marian coat of arms and motto *Totus tuus* — "all for you"). In addition, he has consistently spoken of, taught about, and directed the attention of the whole Church toward the Mother of God. He proclaimed a special Marian Year which began on Pentecost Sunday 1987 and ended on the Feast of the Assumption in 1988. Looking forward with great anticipation to the second millenium celebration of Christ's birth, the Holy Father issued the encyclical letter *Redemptoris Mater* on the Solemnity of the Annunciation in 1987 in order to re-orient the Church "toward the sign of the Woman, toward the correctly defined female dimension of the Church."[19] Such a re-orientation would itself bring about a "new openness for the Spirit's creative power and our transformation into the image and likeness of Christ, whose presence alone can give direction and hope to history."[20] This Marian encyclical of Pope John Paul II also resonates with Lewisian themes. Let us consider some examples.

The most prevalent similarity between the theology of C. S. Lewis and that of Pope John Paul II in *Redemptoris Mater* regards their understanding of the centrality of the Incarnation in the economy of salvation and the role played by the Blessed Virgin Mary in that economy. Basing his reflections on the text of Galatians 4:4-6, the Holy Father begins by saying "The Mother of the Redeemer has a precise place in the plan of salvation, for 'when the time had fully come, God sent forth his Son, born of woman' " (RM 1). In the Incarnation, "Christ and Mary are indissolubly joined" (RM 1). According to the Pope, Mary's presence in history is unique because of her role in the Incarnation and in the plan of God which is "the central reality of Revelation and of faith" (RM 3). Indeed, the Holy Father writes, "One cannot think of the reality of the Incarnation without referring to Mary" (RM 5). In turn, the Incarnation itself enables the Church to more profoundly understand "the mystery of the Mother of the Incarnate Word" (RM 4).

A second Lewisian theological theme which is also referred to in *Redemptoris Mater* is that of the continuity which exists between the Supernatural and the natural order. Lewis is always looking for an entree into the Supernatural world through the material order. The womb of Mary provides precisely that entree. The Pope writes, "... in Mary's *fiat*, first at the Annunciation and then fully at the foot of the Cross, an *interior space* was reopened within humanity which the eternal Father can fill 'with every blessing' " (RM 28). This signifies the re-establishment of a continuity or, if you will, a covenant, between God and the natural order which had been broken due to sin and is now restored in Jesus Christ. Christ is the "continuity" between God and humankind; it is Christ — the Word made flesh — who fills the womb of the Virgin, who occupies that "interior space." Lewis did not deny the value of the material order, as we shall see, and that is why for him, as for the Pope, the Incarnation is the defining moment of salvation history.

A fourth major Lewisian theme referred to in the encyclical is obedience. We have said that Lewis "loved obedience," and the Pope writes:

> Indeed, at the Annunciation Mary entrusted herself to God completely, with the 'full submission of intellect and will,' manifesting 'the obedience of faith' to him who spoke to her through his messenger ... by accepting this announcement, Mary was to become the 'Mother of the Lord,' and the divine mystery of the Incarnation was to be accomplished in her.... (RM 13)

Finally, it is clear that Pope John Paul II sees in Mary's femininity and maternity the archetypical model for the Church's own spousal quality and motherhood (RM 1) — a model of fruitful virginity and the fecundity which results from a life overshadowed by the Holy Spirit. The Church is the Spirit-filled community. Mary as the archetypical figure for femininity, motherhood, and the Church fits well with Lewis's understanding that masculine and feminine archetypes have application and meaning for all of created reality.

d. *Mulieris Dignitatem*

The Apostolic Letter, *Mulieris Dignitatem*, of Pope John Paul II was also issued during the occasion of the Marian Year in 1988.

As its title suggests, this letter is on "The Dignity and Vocation of Women." A careful reading of this document will show it to be replete with theological points and reflections which resonate with at least three of the five central themes of C. S. Lewis as presented in our first chapter. The letter was written in response to a recommendation from the 1987 Assembly of the Synod of Bishops for "a further study of the anthropological and theological bases that are needed in order to solve the problems connected with the meaning and dignity of being a woman and being a man" (MD 1).

Lewis's central theme of masculine and feminine archetypes of reality and the relationship between the two finds strong resonance in the document. In an attempt to respond the Synod's request, the Holy Father provides us with a definition of human being and he elaborates on the meaning and purpose of human life. "To be human means to be called to interpersonal communion ... the whole of human history unfolds within the context of this call" (MD 7). He goes on to say:

> Man — whether man or woman — is the only being among the creatures of the visible world that God the Creator "has willed its own sake"; that creature is thus a person. Being a person means striving towards self-realization (the Council speaks of self-discovery), which can only be achieved "through a sincere gift of self." The model for this interpretation of the person is God himself as Trinity, as a communion of Persons. To say that man is created in the image and likeness of God means that man is called to exist "for" others, to become a gift. (MD 7)

We will see how this relational "I — Thou" concept as a definition of personhood is much taken up by Lewis in his writings. This relationality which culminates in the unity of the Trinity (an "original unity") has been broken in the world by sin. In its state of "original unity," humankind enjoyed "original justice" — "union with God as the source of the unity within his (man's) own 'I,' in the mutual relationship between man and woman (*'communio personorum'*) as well as in regard to the external world, to nature" (MD 9).

Regarding the Blessed Virgin Mary, John Paul II tells us that she has attained a union with God which exceeds all the expectations of the human spirit (MD 3). In light of Mary's place in the economy of salvation he writes, regarding womanhood:

> the "fullness of time" manifests the extraordinary dignity of the "woman" ... this dignity consists in the supernatural elevation to union with God in Jesus Christ, which determines the ultimate finality of the existence of every person both on earth and in eternity. From this point of view, the "woman" is the representative and the archetype of the whole human race: she represents the humanity which belongs to all human beings, both men and women. On the other hand, however, the event at Nazareth highlights a form of union with the living God which can only belong to the "woman," Mary: the union between mother and son. The Virgin of Nazareth truly becomes the Mother of God. (MD 4)

Here, Mary is understood as the archetype of not only the feminine but of all humanity. The new covenant of humanity's union with God in the blood of Jesus Christ begins with a woman. The Pope continues:

> Herein lies the absolute originality of the Gospel: many times in the Old Testament, in order to intervene in the history of his people, God addressed himself to women, as in the case of the mothers of Samuel and Samson. However, to make his covenant with humanity, he addressed himself only to men: Noah, Abraham, and Moses. At the beginning of the New Covenant ... there is a woman ... the Virgin of Nazareth. It is a sign that points to the fact that "in Jesus Christ," "there is neither male nor female" (Galatians 3:28). In Christ the mutual opposition between man and woman — which is the inheritance of original sin — is essentially overcome. "For you are all one in Jesus Christ," St. Paul will write. (MD 11)

A second major Lewisian thematic is the centrality of the Incarnation, of which we have spoken above. Once again, this theme finds full resonance in the document we are presently considering. *Mulieris Dignitatem* sets forth a theological anthropology which attempts to shed light on the meaning and dignity of womanhood. It is noted by the Holy Father that while the eternal truth about the human being is expressed in the protology of the Genesis narrative ("God created man in his own image, in the image of God he created him; male and female he created them" — Genesis 1:27), it remains a mystery which only takes on light in the Incarnate Word, since "Christ fully reveals man to himself and makes his supreme calling clear" (MD 2). The Blessed Virgin Mary has a special role in this revelation — she is that "woman" who is the mother of Christ.

While the eternal truth about the human person finds expression in the Genesis narrative, it is the event of the Incarnation which marks "the turning point of man's history on earth, understood as salvation history" (MD 3). Bridging the old creation in Adam with the new creation in Christ, St. Paul refers to the Mother of the Incarnate Word as "woman" rather than using her own name "Mary" so that the "woman" of the Incarnation (Mary) would coincide with the "woman" of the Proto-evangelium in Genesis 3:15. The Holy Father points out that this is done in order to highlight the centrality of the Incarnation in the economy of salvation and the place of "woman" in this event — in particular the woman Mary. In fact, he writes,

> The sending of this Son, one in substance, with the Father, as a man "born of woman," constitutes the culminating and definitive point of God's self-revelation to humanity. This self-revelation is salvific in character ... a woman is to be found at the center of this salvific event. (MD 3)

Thus the centrality of the Incarnation and the woman's place in it manifests the extraordinary dignity of the woman. In this, the woman Mary represents the humanity which belongs to all human beings, both men and women. (MD 4)

Commenting on how this dignity is particularly feminine in character, and also resonating with the Lewisian theme of the continuity between nature and Supernature, the Holy Father speaks about Mary's status as the one who is "full of grace":

> Grace never casts nature aside nor cancels it out, but rather perfects it and ennobles it. Therefore, the "fullness of grace" that was granted to the Virgin of Nazareth, with a view to the fact that she would become 'Theotokos,' also signifies the fullness of the perfection of 'what is characteristic of woman,' of 'what is feminine.' Here we find ourselves, in a sense, at the culminating point, the archetype, of the personal dignity of women. (MD 5)

This document certainly resonates with Lewis's major thematic on masculine and feminine archetypes, as we shall see in our consideration of his works.

A third area of agreement can be seen in a consideration once again of Mary's free obedience as a sincere gift of self to Christ. Mary's obedience, openness, and receptivity to the Divine initiatives in her life constitute the hallmark of what we have called the "Marian attitude." This is the attitude which is quintessentially Christian. *Mulieris Dignitatem* makes it clear that Mary's faithful obedience to God's word at the Annunciation (her *fiat*) is an exercise of her free will and not the result of divine coercion:

> ... through her response of faith Mary exercises her free will and thus fully shares with her personal and feminine 'I' in the event of the Incarnation. With her 'fiat,' Mary becomes the authentic subject of that union with God which was realized in the mystery of the Incarnation of the Word ... All of God's action in human history at all times respects the free will of the human 'I.' (MD 4)

This "freedom" is always understood in Catholic theological anthropology in the context of service: "The Son of Man came not to be served but to serve" (Mark 10:45). It is grace which impels the creature to participate in the Son's messianic service: "... Mary takes her place within Christ's messianic service. It is precisely this service which constitutes the very foundation of that Kingdom in which 'to serve means to reign' " (MD 5). Mary's obedient service to the divine initiatives in her life is a result of that "fullness of grace" which preconditions the fullness of human freedom.

Mary's obedience is antithetical to the disobedience of Eve. Pope John Paul II takes up the thematic of the Eve-Mary parallel in such a way as to illuminate "the new beginning" of the dignity and vocation of women (MD 11) as it takes shape in the person of the Blessed Virgin Mary. Mary, in virtue of her Immaculate Conception, is able to go beyond the limits imposed by original sin. In Mary we have "a return to that 'beginning' in which one finds the 'woman' as she was intended to be in creation, and therefore in the eternal mind of God: in the bosom of the most holy Trinity" (MD 11). How was "woman" intended to be in the original creation? The woman's "openness" in conceiving and giving birth to a child is an expression of the scriptural ethos which maintains that the human person "cannot fully find himself except through a sincere gift of self" (MD 18). This is the essential indication of what it means to be human. The Pope continues:

> Motherhood implies from the beginning a special openness to the new person: and this is precisely the woman's 'part.' In this openness, in conceiving and giving birth to a child, the woman 'discovers herself through a sincere gift of self' ... Mary's words at the Annunciation — 'Let it be to me according to your word' — signify the woman's readiness for the gift of self and her readiness to accept a new life. (MD 18)

There is no doubt in my mind that Lewis would agree with the theological anthropology presented in *Mulieris Dignitatem*.

e. The *Catechism Of The Catholic Church*

Mary is a figure who bridges the Old and New Testament, summing up in herself the messianic hopes and desires of ancient Israel and fulfilling in herself those hopes and desires in the Incarnation of the Word. The *Catechism* says that God formed Israel in order to recognize Him and serve Him and look for the promised Savior:

> After the Patriarchs, God formed Israel as His people by freeing them from slavery in Egypt. He established with them the covenant of Mount Sinai and, through

Moses, gave them his law so that they would recognize him and serve him as the one living and true God, the provident Father and just judge, and so that they would look for the promised Savior (CCC 623).

We should note the *Catechism's* emphasis that, according to Scripture, "God forms his people in the hope of salvation, in the expectation of a new and everlasting Covenant intended for all, to be written on their hearts" (CCC 64). God gives hope to Israel and expectation for a new Covenant. God also graced Israel with an understanding of his merciful love: "And thanks to the prophets Israel understood that it was again out of love that God never stopped saving them and pardoning their unfaithfulness and sins" (CCC 218). This revelation of God to Israel is simultaneously a revelation about the vocation and truth of the human person, who is made in the image and likeness of God (CCC 2085). The human person discovers that his purpose for being lies in entering into a covenant relationship with the God of love. With what can be considered to be Marian overtones, the *Catechism* also says "Man's vocation is to make God manifest by acting in conformity with his creation 'in the image and likeness of God'" (CCC 2085). We can consider this statement as having Marian overtones because this vocation, of course, took unique shape in Mary's life. The Blessed Virgin Mary is situated directly in the line of Israel's hope and expectation for a new Covenant, and she discovers the ultimate purpose of her life — to be *Theotokos*: God-bearer — within the context of her relationship with the God of love and mercy, as is so beautifully expressed in the *Magnificat*.

In his book *Mary in the Mystery of the Covenant*, Ignace de la Potterie indicates that "joy" and "desire" are constitutive elements of Mary's attitude. Referring to Luke's Annunciation scene (1:26-38), he writes:

> The Greek word "*chaire*" in effect can have two meanings. It can be a simple salutation: "Hello," but it can also have a stronger meaning, a more pregnant meaning of an invitation to joy, "Rejoice" ... it seems practically certain that Luke had to be thinking here of an invitation to joy.[21]

Ignace de la Potterie also notes that this invitation to joy is characteristically addressed to the eschatological Zion as an invitation to rejoice in a future salvation.[22] The Greek Fathers have traditionally interpreted the word of the angel to Mary as an invitation to joy.[23] The same joy motif resounds throughout the whole infancy narrative of Luke, in the "fiat" of Mary, in the words of Elizabeth in the Visitation scene ("Behold, from the moment your greeting reached my ears the child in my womb leapt for joy" — Luke 1:44) and in the words of Mary as she begins to utter the *Magnificat* ("My soul magnifies the Lord and my spirit rejoices in God my savior" — Luke 1:46).[24] In very insightful fashion, de la Potterie concludes:

> It is clear from the very first words of the Angel there is already an echo of the theme of the "Daughter of Zion." The joy which was announced by the prophets in the Old Testament to the people of Israel — the Woman Zion — diffuses itself and comes to be focused on one particular woman, Mary, who unites in her person, so to speak, the desires and the hopes of all the people of Israel.[25]

C. S. Lewis was no exegete, but I am not surprised at a similar statement which he made, particularly with regard to the vicarious nature of God's way of working salvation history:

> One people picked out of the whole earth; that people purged and proved again and again. Some are lost in the desert before they reach Palestine; some stay in Babylon; some become indifferent. The whole thing narrows and narrows, until at last it comes down to a little point, small as the point of a spear — a Jewish girl at her prayers. That is what the whole of human nature has narrowed down to before the Incarnation takes place. Very unlike what we expected, but, of course, not in the least unlike what seems, in general, as shown by nature, to be God's way of working.[26]

By studying the theme of Mary as "Daughter of Zion," exegetes have come to understand "the person of Mary as representative of Israel's perfect response to the covenant established by God on

Sinai."[27] The desire of all of Israel for salvation has come to reside powerfully in Mary,[28] and joy in that salvation reaches a crescendo in the Magnificat. By favoring the symbolism of Mary as Daughter of Zion or Israel personified, as some exegetes do,[29] we can say with Bertrand Buby, "Zion becomes a powerful symbol for the presence of God in Israel. Holiness, security, salvation, and joy are all embodied in the theme and symbol of Zion."[30] Cardinal Ratzinger agrees with the equation of Mary with the Daughter of Zion when he writes:

> Perhaps Laurentin is not entirely off the mark when he finds the whole scene of the visitation constructed as a parallel to the homecoming of the Ark of the Covenant; thus the leaping of the child (John) continues David's ecstatic joy at the guarantee of God's nearness. Be that as it may, something is expressed here that has been almost entirely lost in our century and nonetheless belongs to the heart of faith; essential to it is the joy in the Word become man, the dance before the Ark of the Covenant, in self-forgetful happiness, by one who has recognized God's salvific nearness. Only against this background can Marian devotion be comprehended. Transcending all problems, Marian devotion is the rapture of joy over the true, indestructible Israel; it is a blissful entering into the joy of the *Magnificat* and thereby it is the praise of him to whom the Daughter Zion owes her whole self and whom she bears, the true, incorruptible, indestructible Ark of the Covenant.[31]

Accepting the symbolism of Mary as Daughter of Zion or Israel, we perceive that the Chosen People's desire for intimate communion with Yahweh and Israel's joy in the salvific nearness of God are two categories which reach fulfillment in the life of the Blessed Virgin Mary. This fundamental principle of holiness as union with God is beautifully summed up in a paragraph from the *Catechism* on "The Mystery of the Church":

> In the Church this communion of men with God, in the "love [that] never ends," is the purpose which governs everything in her that is a sacramental means, tied to this passing world. "[The Church's] structure is totally

ordered to the holiness of Christ's members. And holiness is measured according to the 'great mystery' in which the Bride responds with the gift of love to the gift of the Bridegroom." Mary goes before us all in the holiness that is the Church's mystery as "the bride without spot or wrinkle." This is why the "Marian" dimension of the Church precedes the "Petrine" (CCC 773).

i. The Faith Of Mary In the *Catechism Of The Catholic Church*

To bring further precision to the concept of a "Marian attitude," it would be beneficial to briefly consider the faith of Mary as it is explained in the *Catechism*, where it is alluded to more than twenty times.

The overall characteristic of Mary's faith as it is expressed in the *Catechism* is the obedience of that faith. Explicit allusion to Mary's "obedience" is made five times in the text: numbers 144, 148, 494, 511, and 968. The first citation sets the tone. In Part One: "The Profession of Faith," Section One, Chapter Three on "Man's Response to God," number 144 reads as follows:

> To obey (from the Latin *ob — audire*, to "hear or listen to") in faith is to submit freely to the word that has been heard, because its truth is guaranteed by God, who is Truth itself. Abraham is the model of such obedience offered us by Sacred Scripture. The Virgin Mary is its most perfect embodiment (CCC 144).

Obedience, then, is what characterizes Mary's relationship to the Word that she heard at the Annunciation: "Behold, you will conceive in your womb and bear a son, and you shall name him Jesus. He will be great and will be called Son of the Most High" (Luke 1:31-32a). In the end, her obedient response in faith is: "Behold, I am the handmaid of the Lord. May it be done to me according to your word" (Luke 1:38a). The obedience of faith in the giving of her assent at the Annunciation (#148) prompts Mary to give herself entirely to the person and to the work of her Son (#494). Thus does her obedience reverse the disobedience of Eve, making Mary the new mother of the living (#511), a role which continues in the Church (#968). While Mary's was a true "pilgrimage of faith" which walked into the "night of faith" (#165), it is a faith that never wavered from the Annunciation until Calvary (#s 964, 969, 2674). "And so the Church venerates in Mary the purest realization of faith" (#149). Quoting *Lumen Gentium* #63, the *Catechism* speaks of Mary's faith as "unadulterated by any doubt" (#506).

Mary's obedience contains no notion of restraint. Her submission to the Word of God is performed with openness and receptivity. It is the type of faith which "can embrace the mysterious ways of God's almighty power" (#273). Hers was a "free assent" in faith to the announcement of her vocation, made possible because, throughout her life, she was "wholly borne by God's grace" (#490). Even in the face of a lack of understanding of the young Jesus's words to her (Luke 2:49 — the finding of Jesus in the Temple), "Mary and Joseph ... accepted them in faith" (#534). And again, "In the faith of his humble handmaid, the Gift of God found the acceptance he had awaited from the beginning of time" (#2617). Echoing de la Potterie's equation of Mary's lifelong desire for virginity with the grace that was operative in her (cf. footnote #28), the *Catechism* says that "By the Holy Spirit's power and her faith, her virginity became uniquely fruitful" (#723). Her faith is characterized by "adherence to the Father's will, to his Son's redemptive work and to every prompting of the Holy Spirit" (#967).

Thus we see that references to Mary's faith in the *Catechism of the Catholic Church* are characterized by an obedience of free submission to the Word of God, accepting that Word with openness and receptivity. In addition to the desire for intimate communion with God and joy in the salvific nearness of Yahweh, these are the elements which definitively constitute what we are calling a "Marian attitude."

---

1. Gerald O'Collins, S. J. and Edward G. Farrugia, S. J., "Mysticism" in *A Concise Dictionary of Theology*. (New York: Paulist Press, 1991), p. 152.

2. C. S. Lewis, *The Pilgrim's Regress, An Allegorical Apology for Christianity, Reason and Romanticism*. (Grand Rapids, MI: Eerdman's, 1958), p. 167.

3. The "Dogmatic Constitution on the Church," Vatican II, *Lumen Gentium* in Vatican Council II — *The Conciliar and Post Conciliar Documents*, Austin Flannery, O. P., ed. (Collegeville, MN: Liturgical Press, 1975), para. #1, p. 350.

4. Ibid., para. #41, p. 398.

5. Ibid. For a good commentary on the history of this phrase as it underwent revisions by the Conciliar Fathers, see Paolo Molinari and Peter Gumpel, *Il Capitolo VI "De Religiosis" Della Costituzione Dogmatica Sulla Chiesa*. (Milano: Editrice Ancora, 1985), esp. pp. 116-124. Here I translate three insightful paragraphs:

What does the Council intend when it affirms that *one sanctity* is cultivated by all Christians? The answer to this question is not difficult if we keep in mind what was said above — namely that the term "sanctity" means, in the mind of the Council, the union of the faithful with Christ which the Holy Spirit works in the Church. To say that Christian holiness is "one" is thereby equivalent to affirming that the life of union with Christ is radically, fundamentally one. (p. 116)

Sadly, not a few translations of the conciliar texts, not to mention certain popularizations, have largely diffused the erroneous idea that the sanctity of Christians is not only "one," but is also "identical" for all, as if all Christians were called to the "same" sanctity, to the *same* perfection of charity. (p. 118)

The authors quote a section of the "Schema" of the draft document of the dogmatic constitution (*Acta Synodalia*, Vol. II, pars I, pp. 325-326):

Many Fathers (and above all the group of 679) have requested that, once the unity of holiness is affirmed, one teaches also the diversity (of holiness) according to diverse levels. Therefore the new text (the approved document) retains the affirmation that holiness is *one*; but it does not add more, as did the preceding text, that it is also *the same*. In this way the new text implicitly recognizes the diversity (of holiness) according to diverse levels and vocations. (p. 119)

6. For a concise definition and history of the term *Theotokos*, see O'Collins and Farrugia, ibid., p. 242.

7. Luke 1:29, 2:19 and 51, Acts 1:14.

8. Lumen Gentium, para #61, Flannery, ibid., p. 418:

The predestination of the Blessed Virgin as Mother of God was associated with the incarnation of the divine word: in the designs of divine Providence she was the gracious mother of the divine Redeemer here on earth, and above all others and in a singular way the generous associate and humble handmaid of the Lord.

9. M. J. Scheeben, *Mariology*. (St. Louis: B. Herder Book Co., 1948), p. 30.

10. Otto Semmelroth, *Mary Archetype of the Church*. (New York: Sheed and Ward, Inc., 1963), pp. 7-8.

11. Roberts, Alexander & Donaldson, James, eds. *The Ante-Nicene Fathers*. Vol. I. (Grand Rapids, MI: Wm. B. Eerdmans Publishing Co., 1973).

12. Ibid., *Dial.* 45, p. 217.

13. Ibid., *Dial.* 100, p. 249.

14. Semmelroth, p. 13.

15. Ibid., p. 32.

16. Ibid., pp. 83-5.

17. Laurentin, Rene in *Mary in Faith and Life in the New Age of the Church*. (Dayton: International Marian Research Institute, Marian Seminar 1980), p. 173.

18. Ibid., p. 138.

19. Ratzinger, Joseph Cardinal in "Introduction." *Mary: God's Yes to Man, John Paul's Encyclical Redemptoris Mater*. (San Francisco: Ignatius Press, 1988), p. 39.

20. Ibid.

21. Ignace de la Potterie, *Mary in the Mystery of the Covenant*. (New York: Alba House, 1992), p. 14.

22. Ibid.

23. Ibid., p. 15.

24. Ibid., p. 16.

25. Ibid.

26. C. S. Lewis, "The Grand Miracle" in *God in the Dock*, p. 84.

27. Bertrand Buby, SM, *Mary of Galilee, Vol. II, Woman of Israel — Daughter of Zion.* (New York: Alba House, 1995), p. 59.

28. In his treatment of Mary's questions to the angel, "How shall this be done: since I do not know man?" (Luke 1:34) de la Potterie equates Mary's desire for virginity with the grace that was operative in her. de la Potterie writes,

> ... we do not think that it is a question of a conscious decision to keep one's virginity. That would be putting too much into the text. At this moment in salvation history that would be an anachronism. It is rather a question of orientation, of a profound attraction to a virginal way of life, a secret desire for virginity, proved and existentially experienced by Mary, but which could not yet take the form of a decision, because that was impossible in the milieu in which she lived. If we accept this interpretation, we will better understand the paradoxical situation in which Mary found herself. She is married to Joseph, because she followed the customs of her time and of her milieu. But the desire of her soul orients itself in another way. This interior paradox in which she finds herself receives a marvelous solution when the angel announces to her that it will be in a virginal way that she is to become the Mother of the Messiah, the Son of God. By operation of the Holy Spirit, virginity and maternity will exist side by side in a manner still full of mystery. (p. 27)

and again,

> From her youth — under the impulse of the grace of God which accompanied her from the first years of her life — Mary lived in the perspective of virginity. Even before her Son later proposed it as an ideal, Mary already existentially lived virginity ... This is then the "grace" which gives us the key to everything; it permits us to explain the entire content of the angelic annunciation to Mary: her desire for virginity, her preservation from sin and concupiscence, but also the grace of her divine maternity and finally of her consent full of joyful enthusiasm for the design of God. (p. 29)

29. cf. Buby, pp. 57-69.

30. Ibid., p. 67.

31. Joseph Cardinal Ratzinger, *Daughter Zion.* (San Francisco: Ignatius Press, 1983), pp. 81-2.

Chapter Four
The Marian Attitude In C. S. Lewis

Union with God is achieved by openness, receptivity, and obedience to His Word. It is a free submission of the will in accord with an intimate desire for communion with God and the experience of rapturous joy over the salvific nearness of Yahweh. These are the qualities which constitute the Marian attitude which is the quintessentially Christian attitude. Having this attitude is a fundamental prerequisite for Christian holiness, and Lewis makes this point clear in his writings. In order to appreciate that which Lewis believed should be the ultimate object of the Christian's openness, receptivity, and obedience, it is most profitable to journey with him as his awareness of this Supernatural reality grows as expressed in his autobiography, *Surprised by Joy*. We will discover that by tracing the "tracks" left by his experiences of "joy," he finds imprints of the Divine initiative in his life. He examines his "desire" for experiences of joy and discovers that the desire itself is greater than any fulfillment of it which he has experienced on earth. He comes to realize that it is therefore a desire for communion with a reality beyond himself — a desire rooted in the beyond and therefore experienced by him as gift, but which expresses itself in human experience. In this way, he is ultimately led to an acceptance of the Incarnation — the quintessential human experience of the "Desired of all nations."

In his autobiography, Lewis speaks of learning about *sehnsucht* — or longing — for some reality which was far off and unattainable. What was the object of this "longing," this "desire"? What was it a longing for? As a child, it was not a longing for another world, because, he writes, "My childhood ... was not in the least other-worldly."[1] Later on in childhood, remembering the experience of longing which accompanied his viewing of his brother's toy garden, Lewis speaks about experiencing a longing or a desire for something which he cannot yet define. He called it a "longing for a longing" which was in itself quite fleeting. In comparison, however, anything else in his experience was quite insignificant.[2] Another glimpse of this same experience came through reading *Squirrel Nutkin* by Beatrix Potter. Here he calls it for the first time an intimate desire, "quite different from ordinary life and even from ordinary pleasure; something ... 'in another dimension.' "[3] Then, through poetry, he became fond of a pleasure which came "like a voice from far more distant regions"[4] — again, a fleeting experience which he quickly fell out of. All these seem to have been rather generic, non-religious experiences, but not equitable simply with "happiness" or "pleasure."

As for that which is common to these three experiences of "longing," he writes that it is

> an unsatisfied desire which is itself more desirable than any other satisfaction. I call it Joy, which is here a technical term and must be sharply distinguished both from Happiness and from Pleasure. Joy (in my sense) has indeed one characteristic, and one only, in common with them; the fact that anyone who has experienced it will want it again. Apart from that, and considered only in its quality, it might almost equally well be called a particular kind of unhappiness or grief. But then it is a kind we want. I doubt whether anyone who has tasted it would ever, if both were in his power, exchange it for all the pleasures in the world. But then Joy is never in our own power and pleasure often is.[5]

It is significant to note that Lewis identifies his experiences of joy as being outside of and beyond the control of the human person. Thus early in life he recognizes it as a gifted reality.

As mentioned previously, Lewis says that he became an "effective believer" first at his childhood school in Hertfordshire, where he attended high "Anglo-Catholic" church every Sunday and where he first learned the doctrines of Christianity. This was the beginning of his attempts at prayer, Bible-reading, and the obeying of his conscience. From this beginning he would eventually fall back into atheism during his later school days.

In later childhood, Lewis assumed a great interest in fairy tales. Throughout his childhood, he experienced a continued growth in the power of his imagination. Though it often was not a romantic or poetic imagination — it was more often what he called "almost astonishingly prosaic"[6] — we can see that these were the beginnings in him of his ability to write tremendously imaginative children's stories.

Lewis identifies the loss of his Christianity with his early teen years at "Chartres," a college preparatory school which he attended. For it was here that his fascination with the world of imagination and fantasy came alive, but not in exactly the most wholesome way. He turned his attention to the occult. It is interesting to note that at this time Lewis admits to suffering from a form of religious scrupulosity, and that this was no minor factor in his drifting away from Christianity. He says:

> I set myself a standard. No clause of my prayer was to be allowed to pass muster unless it was accompanied by what I called a "realization," by which I meant a certain vividness of the imagination and the affections ... The thing threatened to become an infinite regress ... Had I pursued the same road much further I think I should have gone mad.[7]

Reason enough to stop pursuing the faith! Lewis then goes on to elaborate on other more conscious motives for leaving Christianity behind, including the reading of the classics, like Virgil, and the idea that since the mass of religious ideas presented therein should be so easily dismissed as Pagan, why not do the same with Christianity? This experience would later prompt Lewis to dedicate much of his apologetics to showing how Christianity fulfilled Paganism or Paganism prefigured Christianity.

Lewis describes the "boyhood" of his early teens as a dry, desert period. Even joy — the pangs of "inconsolable longing" — disappeared from his life. The return of it came around the age of fifteen with reading the title of Wagner's classical opera *Siegfried and the Twilight of the Gods*:

> ... The distance of the Twilight of the Gods and the distance of my own past Joy, both unattainable, flowed together into a single, unendurable sense of desire and loss, which suddenly became one with the loss of the whole experience, which, as I now stared round that dusty schoolroom like a man recovering from unconsciousness, had already vanished, had eluded me at the very moment when I could first say *It is*. And at once I knew (with fatal knowledge) that to "have it again" was the supreme and only important object of desire.[8]

This "other-worldliness" he called "Pure Northerness ... a vision of huge, clear spaces hanging above the Atlantic in the endless twilight of Northern summer, remoteness, severity ..."[9] Despite the fact that this was still a quite a — religious phenomenon, he tells us that it taught him "adoration," or

> some kind of quite disinterested self-abandonment to an object which securely claimed this by simply being the object it was ... Sometimes I can almost think that I was sent back to the false gods there to acquire some capacity for worship against the day when the true God should recall me to Himself.[10]

Next, and still quite the atheist, he would be off to college. What seems to have continuously characterized his most formative experiences, however understood at the time, was that "desire" for something far beyond himself and quite unattainable, even if believed for a time to be purely imaginative. The object of it was beyond him, but the desire for it was within him. Lewis describes his years at Wyvern College as having been "sick with desire; that sickness better than health."[11] His imaginative experiences were now to be counter-balanced by a stretch of time spent with his father's own one-time headmaster and his brother's tutor, Mr. Kirkpatrick — the "Great Knock" — as Lewis's father called him, a master of practicality and a confirmed atheist. Here, Lewis acquired a certain sense of disinterest in social life. He called it "a settled, calm, Epicurean life"[12] almost entirely selfish, but different from self-concern or self-pity. During this time, Lewis grows close to his friend Arthur Greeves, who helps Lewis to develop an appreciation for what Lewis called "homeliness" or the pleasure of simple experiences: weather, food, the family, the neighborhood, and things found in nature — "out-of-door scenes." I think that the development of this appreciation in Lewis is critical to his understanding of the potential sacramentality of everyday life and its experiences — that is, the access life can afford to the "northerness" which was the object of what was until now the imaginative experiences of "desire" or "longing" of which he was still having many stabs. A quote is here necessary:

> Often he (Arthur) recalled my eyes from the horizon just to look through a hole in a hedge, to see nothing more than a farmyard in its mid-morning solitude, and perhaps a gray cat squeezing its way under a barn door, or a bent old woman with a wrinkled, motherly face coming back with an empty bucket from the pigsty. But best of all we liked it when the Homely and the unhomely met in sharp juxtaposition; if a little kitchen garden ran steeply up a narrowing enclave of fertile ground surrounded by outcroppings and furze, or some shivering quarry pool under a moonrise could be seen on our left, and on our right the smoking chimney and lamplit window of a cottage that was just settling down for the night.[13]

Thus does Lewis first begin to really appreciate the coincidence between the "Homely" and the "unhomely" — between the simple, close to home and the majestic, far away; between what is within our grasp and what is beyond; between nature and Supernature — an exceedingly important development in the life and thought of C. S. Lewis.

Lewis ultimately realizes that his imaginative longing for "joy" had become a longing for a state of his own mind, and this was a "deadly error." He writes, "Only when your whole attention and desire are fixed on something else — whether a distant mountain or the past, or the gods of Asgard — does the thrill arise. It is the by-product. Its very existence pre-supposes that you desire not it, but something other and outer."[14] This other-worldly longing, however, was as yet "unbaptized." But this would happen soon.

Lewis relates an "encounter with holiness" in his reading of *Phantastes, A Faerie Romance* by George Macdonald. In fact, he locates in the reading of this book an experience of "continuity" between nature and Supernature which has the effect of "baptizing" his imagination. He writes of this experience:

> Thus, when the great moments came I did not break away from the woods and cottages that I read of to seek some bodiless light shining beyond them, but gradually, with a swelling continuity (like the sun at midmorning burning through a fog) I found the light shining on those woods and cottages, and then on my own past life, and on the quiet room where I sat and on my old teacher where he nodded above his little *Tacitus*. For I now perceived that while the air of the new region made all my erotic and radical perversions of Joy look like sordid trumpery, it had no such disenchanting power over the bread upon the table or the coals in the grate. That was the marvel. Up till now each visitation of Joy had left the common world momentarily a desert — "The first touch of the earth went nigh to kill." Even when real clouds or trees had been the material of the vision, they had been so only by reminding me of another world; and I did not like the return to ours. But now I saw the bright shadow coming out of the book into the real world and resting there, transforming all common things and yet itself unchanged. Or, more accurately, I saw the common things drawn into the bright shadow. *Unde hoc mihi?* In the depth of my disgraces, in the then invincible ignorance of my intellect, all this

> was given me without asking, even without consent. That night my imagination was, in a certain sense, baptized; the rest of me, not unnaturally, took longer. I had not the faintest notion what I had let myself in for by buying *Phantastes*.[15]

Because of his new-found and tremendous appreciation of all that Arthur Greeves would have called "homely" (the familiar, the near-at-hand, the home-spun, the natural), this critical passage in Lewis's autobiography lays the groundwork for a beautiful theology of the Incarnation wherein the Divine "pitches his tent" (John 1:14) in the midst of the world of his own creation.

All this happened by the time Lewis was first admitted to Oxford in the summer of 1917, soon after which he went off to war, and was wounded in France in April, 1918. He returned to Oxford in January, 1919, and continued his education in the appreciation of the "homely" by his exposure to one who would become a life-long friend, A. K. Hamilton Jenkin. By his own admission, Lewis not only learned from Jenkin a greater appreciation for the "homely," but also an ability to "surrender" to it:

> He continued (what Arthur had begun) my education as a seeing, listening, smelling, receptive creature. Arthur had had his preference for the Homely. But Jenkin seemed to be able to enjoy everything; even ugliness. I learned from him that we should attempt a total surrender to whatever atmosphere was offering itself at the moment; in a squalid town to seek out those very places where its squalor rose to grimness and almost grandeur, on a dismal day to find the most dismal and dripping wood, on a windy day to seek the windiest ridge. There was no Betjemannic irony about it; only a serious, yet gleeful, determination to rub one's nose in the very quiddity of each thing, to rejoice in its being (so magnificently) what it was.[16]

Lewis, however, still had no attraction to theism. The so-called "stabs of Joy" or experiences of desire for the other and outer which arose from majestic experiences of nature as well as from "homely" experiences of life he labeled as aesthetic rather than religious experiences. During this time, the influence of the Anthroposophy of certain Oxford friends like Owen Barfield and A. C. Harwood was unavoidable. Lewis says that this influence destroyed his own "chronological snobbery" (the attitude that would lead him to believe that because things Supernatural belonged to an earlier and ignorant age, they are therefore less credible) and his belief in the rock-bottom reality of nature as a final end. They taught him that his own mind — the same mind which appreciated nature and the reality of the senses — was itself at least part of another rock-bottom reality, not conditioned by nature. He writes, "I must admit that mind was no late-come epiphenomenon; that the whole universe was, in the last resort, mental; that our own logic was participation in a cosmic *Logos*."[17] Although the influence of Anthroposophy merely brought Lewis to a more sophisticated form of his old occultism, theism was to be the next step, and it arrived in the line of Lewis's ability to appreciate as Divine that other-worldly reality which revealed itself through created reality. His ability to appreciate the Divine was rooted in that "northerness" beyond the natural world which expressed itself as the "stuff" of that special desire (*sehnsucht*) which the human person is capable of experiencing as moments of "joy." It was during his fourth year reading English at Oxford that Lewis sensed challenges to his non-Theistic belief in an "Absolute" of cosmic logic. These challenges came from friendships with Christians like Nevill Coghill and later, while on the Oxford English faculty, with J. R. R. Tolkien. Lewis eventually comes to this important conclusion about "Joy," always a constitutive element of his perception of reality:

> Joy was a desire ... But a desire is turned not to itself but to its object ... The form of the desired is in the desire ... It is the object which makes the desire itself either desirable or hateful. I perceived that just as I had been wrong in supposing that I really desired the Garden of Hesperides, so also I had been equally wrong in supposing that I desired Joy itself, considered simply as an event in my mind ... All the value lay in that of which Joy was the desiring. And that object, quite clearly, was no state of my own mind or body at all ... I thus understood that in deepest solitude there is a road right out of

> the self, a commerce with something which, by refusing to identify itself with any object of the senses, or anything whereof we have biological or social need, or anything imagined, or any state of our own minds, proclaims itself sheerly objective ... the naked Other, imageless (though our imagination salutes it with a hundred images), unknown, undefiled, desired.[18]

And equally important, Lewis now shows the vital connection between the human person and the "naked Other" of desire:

> In so far as we really are at all, we have, so to speak, a root in the Absolute, which is the utter reality. And that is why we experience Joy: we yearn, rightly, for that unity which we can never reach except by ceasing to be the separate phenomenal beings called "we." Joy was not a deception. Its visitations were rather the moments of clearest consciousness we had, when we became aware of our fragmentary and phantasmal nature and ached for that impossible reunion which would annihilate us.[19]

It was now left for Lewis to come to the realization that this "union" for which all human hearts ache was, in fact, not impossible to achieve. And the initiative in achieving this union lay not with him, but in the "Other":

> Even if my own philosophy were true, how could the initiative lie on my side? My own analogy ... suggested the opposite: if Shakespeare and Hamlet could ever meet, it must be Shakespeare's doing. Hamlet could initiate nothing. Perhaps, even now, my Absolute Spirit still differed in some way from the God of religion. The real issue was not, or not yet, there. The real terror was that if you seriously believed in such a "God" or "Spirit" as I admitted, a wholly new situation developed. As the dry bones shook and came together in that dreadful valley of Ezekiel's, so now a philosophical theorem, cerebrally entertained, began to stir and heave and throw off its grave-clothes, and stood upright and became a living presence. I was to be allowed to play at philosophy no longer. It might, as I say, still be true

> that my "Spirit" differed in some way from "the God of popular religion." My adversary waived the point. It sank into utter unimportance. He would not argue about it. He only said, "I am the Lord"; "I am that I am"; "I am."[20]

It seems, finally, as if God had invited himself into Lewis's life, and Lewis finally opened the door to him: "In the Trinity term of 1929 I gave in, and admitted that God was God, and knelt and prayed: perhaps that night the most dejected and reluctant convert in all of England."[21] Thus does Lewis conclude a reasoned and gifted journey to Theism via the route of "joy" and "desire."

The ultimate step to Christianity is a beautiful tribute to the Incarnation:

> Every step I had taken, from the Absolute to "Spirit" and from Spirit to "God," had been a step toward the more concrete, the more immanent, the more compulsive ... To accept the Incarnation was a further step in the same direction. It brings God nearer, or near in a new way.[22]

Thus did the God of his heart and soul's desire reveal Himself to C. S. Lewis in the person of Jesus Christ. All in all, it was a reasoned journey to faith, a philosophical journey, and — in the end — a gifted journey. The "visitations" of joy throughout his life were all preparatory to his acceptance of the Desired One's arrival in the flesh. It was all, for Lewis, a "pilgrim's regress" back to that source of unity and being from which his own life and all lives were originally generated. But the "way back," the "regress," was through the world, through the flesh, via the Incarnation. The "how" of this return to participation in Divine life is all the topic of Lewis's doctrinal and apologetic works. But the category of "union with God" achieved through experiences of joy effected in the material order constitutes his comprehension of Christian holiness, as has been made quite clear in his popular autobiography.

Lewis's understanding of "joy" and "desire" became the theological filter through which he viewed his life's experiences and his growth in union with God. Consider his admitted attraction to the writings of George Herbert. He was reading Herbert just before his conversion. He appreciated Herbert's ability to interpret the quality of daily life as it is lived from moment to moment. Herbert's writings were intensely Christocentric and sacramental. In the Incarnation, for Herbert, Christ had become the sacrament of divinity in human disguise, and with him all of the created order. In the poem "To All Angels and Saints" (op. cit., ch. 2) Herbert emphasizes the "materiality" or the humanity which Jesus took from His Mother ("Thou art the holy mine, whence came the gold"). In a similar manner, Lewis speaks of the humanity which Jesus took from Mary in a beautiful passage in his *Reflections on the Psalms*:

> I think, too, it will do us no harm to remember that, in becoming Man, He bowed his neck beneath the sweet yoke of a heredity and early environment. Humanly speaking, He would have learned His style, if from no one else (but it was all about Him) from His Mother. "That we should be saved from our enemies and from the hands of all that hate us; to perform the mercy promised to our fathers, and to remember his holy covenant." Here is the same parallelism. (And incidentally, is this the only aspect in which we can say of His human nature "He was His Mother's own son?" There is a fierceness, even a touch of Deborah, mixed with the sweetness in the *Magnificat* to which most painted Madonnas do little justice; matching the frequent severity of His own sayings. I am sure the private life of the holy family was, in many senses, "mild" and "gentle," but perhaps hardly in the way some hymn writers have in mind. One may suspect, on proper occasions, a certain astringency; and all in what people at Jerusalem regarded as a rough north-country dialect.)[23]

C. S. Lewis sees Mary as a *locus* for divine activity in the world. And more than just a *locus*, she offers the materiality of her very self in addition to her consent in faith for participation in this activity. Mary's "yes" at the Annunciation is possible only because she believes in miracles (a virginal pregnancy) and she believes in the possibility of a continuity between Divine life and the material order, which material order ultimately accommodates itself to the miracle. Prescinding from historical-critical debate on the question of the Virgin birth, Lewis, in his apologetic work *Miracles*, points out that both Mary and Joseph must have accepted the idea that the Divine reality could first invade and then be continuous with the created order. He writes:

> ... you will hear people say, "The early Christians believed that Christ was the son of a virgin, but we know that this is a scientific impossibility." Such people seem to have an idea that belief in miracles arose at a period when men were so ignorant of the cause of nature that they did not perceive a miracle to be contrary to it. A moment's thought shows this to be nonsense: and the story of the Virgin Birth is a particularly striking example. When St. Joseph discovered that his fiancee was going to have a baby, he not unnaturally decided to repudiate her. Why? Because he knew just as well as any modern gynecologist that in the ordinary course of nature women do not have babies unless they have lain with men. No doubt the modern gynecologist knows several things about birth and begetting which St. Joseph did not know. But those things do not concern the main point — that a virgin birth is contrary to the course of nature. And St. Joseph obviously knew *that*. In any sense in which it is true to say now, "The thing is scientifically impossible," he would have said the same: the thing always was, and was always known to be, impossible *unless* the regular processes of nature were, in this particular case, being over-ruled or supplemented by something from beyond nature.[24]

The subtitle for Lewis's book *Miracles* is "How God Intervenes in Nature and Human Affairs." His attitude toward all miracles is Marian because it is rooted in his understandings of "the Grand Miracle" to which Mary was so intimately receptive on behalf of all humankind — the Incarnation. Speaking of the drama of human existence and history, Lewis says, "That is why I think this Grand Miracle is the missing chapter in this novel, the chapter on which the whole plot turns; that is why I believe that God really has dived down into the bottom of creation, and has come up bringing the whole redeemed nature on His shoulder."[25] Mary's responsiveness to this type of God's action in history is, for Lewis, a prerequisite for the Incarnation as it occurred. Of God's "selectiveness" in choosing from amongst the created order as the means for humankind's salvation and of Mary's prayerful and obedient response to that selectiveness, Lewis writes:

> We, with our modern democratic and arithmetical presuppositions would so have liked and expected all men to start equal in their search for God. One has the picture of great centripetal roads coming from all directions, with well-disposed people, all meaning the same thing, and getting closer and closer together. How shockingly opposite to that is the Christian story! One people picked out of the whole earth; that people purged and proved again and again. Some are lost in the desert before they reach Palestine; some stay in Babylon; some become indifferent. The whole thing narrows and narrows, until at last it comes down to a little point, small as the point of a spear — a Jewish girl at her prayers. That is what the whole of human nature has narrowed down to before the Incarnation takes place. Very unlike what we expected, but, of course, not in the least unlike what seems, in general, as shown by nature, to be God's way of working.[26]

Lewis is not at all afraid to attribute salvific necessity to the *fiat* of the Blessed Virgin Mary. In his essay "Priestesses in the Church?" cited earlier, wherein he expresses his opposition to the ordination of women in the Anglican Church in part based on his perception of the place of Mary in the New Testament Scriptures, Lewis writes, "All salvation depends on the decision which she made in the words *ecce ancilla*."[27]

For Lewis, receptivity to the revelation of God in the world and openness to revelatory experiences in everyday life (due to an acceptance of the possibility of the miraculous and the way in which, subsequently, nature and Supernature accommodate one another) are essential to the development of a true Christian attitude. And, as we have seen, this is also very much a Marian attitude. Once God's revelation is recognized, it is left for the human person to exercise the obedience of faith which characterized the life of the Blessed Virgin Mary. Lewis's understanding of the nature of such obedience will be treated in detail in the next section.

The Marian Attitude In *Perelandra*

1. An Introduction to "The Space Trilogy"

In "The Space Trilogy" we find what Madeleine L'Engle describes as the "anagogical level" of the writings of C. S. Lewis. Purely fictional, it is not, however, allegorical. Lewis would not want the characters of this trilogy to be seen as fictional representations of some human figures. Rather, the reader is invited to enter into a world of fantasy which contains a depth of reality greater than surface human experiences. Therefore, the figure in *Perelandra* — the second book of the trilogy — which we will describe as having a Marian attitude is not understood by Lewis as the allegorical representation of the historical figure of the Blessed Virgin Mary. Rather, Tinidril — as she is called — is properly understood (to paraphrase Lewis's own description of the lion Aslan in the *Chronicles of Narnia*) as an invention giving an imaginary answer to the question, "What might Mary be like, if there really were a world like Perelandra, and she were chosen to be the mother of all its human inhabitants?"[28]

Before examining the second book of "The Space Trilogy," let us briefly examine the foundations which are laid for it in the first book, *Out of the Silent Planet*, for this book sets up for the reader Lewis's understanding of a deeper level of reality while the second book is a presentation of human action on that level.

Lewis is convinced that there is more to the world and to life than what our senses present to us. This is the truth he attempts to express in imaginary fashion. In *Out of the Silent Planet*, a fantastic tale of interplanetary travel, Ransom, a university philologist, finds himself, through a variety of good-will gestures, on a spaceship with an old schoolmate (Devine) and a scientist (Weston), both of whom come to have major roles in the next two books of the trilogy. The spaceship is headed for "Malacandra" (Mars), where

Weston hopes to begin the human race's conquest of infinity and, perhaps, eternity. Quite immediately, however, Ransom begins to savor "space" not as something to be conquered but rather to be enjoyed for the "heaven" that it really is — brimming with brightness and vitality. From the beginning of the journey, Weston and Ransom are set before us with opposing values and contrary visions of reality. Weston expects that his narrow-minded vision of reality will "fit" with the reality of the other worlds he is visiting. But Ransom is the one who comes to learn that earthly reality is only an image of, or at best, a participation in, a greater reality. The two characters come across creatures on Malacandra which, according to the earthly categories of Weston, are worthy neither of dignity or respect equal to that which is accorded to the human species, and so he has no problem killing them. Ransom, on the other hand, comes to learn from and love these creatures because of his sensitivity to the possibility that human beings are not the only or the highest form of life in the cosmos. There is a greater picture of life into which the human person has been inserted. This concept, in vintage Lewis style, invites the reader to conclude in favor of a reality larger than that of simple human experience — leading the reader to perceive the possibility of a "world behind (or larger than) the world." By expanding the human person's horizons of reality, Lewis wants ultimately to invite the reader to a belief in Supernature, which has been so lost in our own day and age.

A quick overview of this first story in the trilogy is necessary for our understanding. Besides being inhabited by various life forms (*hrossa, seroni, pfifltriggi*), Malacandra is also a stage for the activity of *eldila* (angels), whom humans find it at first difficult to perceive. The "Oyarsa" is the presiding "eldil" or spirit of Malacandra, of which each planet in the solar system has one. These are all presided over by "Maleldil" (God). There is one planetary exception: "Thulcandra" (earth) is "the silent planet," not presided over by a ruling eldil because of the rebellion and fall of one who once presided (in our story, it's called the fall of Lucifer). As a result of having no guiding eldil, Thulcandra has fallen out of communication with Maleldil and the other planets and also has fallen out of step altogether in the "Great Dance of Being" in which the planets participate. Having thus fallen out of communication, it is a "silent planet" from which Ransom has come. Since there is no presiding eldil for Thulcandra, "every one of them (humans) wants to be a little Oyarsa himself."[29] In this way, Lewis makes it clear that he considers *hubris* or pride to be the first and greatest sin. The Oyarsa of Malacandra, having been taught by Maleldil to do so, prevented the fear of death from spreading amongst the creatures of his planet as it did over the humans of Thulcandra. Along with the other Oyarsa, he confined the activity of Thulcandra's fallen Oyarsa to the realms of Thulcandra. It is as a result of the fear of death that Weston feels the need to travel beyond the bounds of the planet Thulcandra in an attempt to conquer the planets of space, to overcome the limits which infinity places on humanity, and thus to provide for the eternal existence of the human race. In the end, the Oyarsa of Malacandra sends Weston, Devine, and Ransom back to Thulcandra — Weston's plans for conquest having been thwarted — with the admonition to Ransom: "you must watch this Weston and this Devine in Thulcandra, if ever you arrive there. They may yet do much evil in, and beyond, your world ... Watch these two bent ones! Be courageous. Fight them."[30]

It is interesting to note how Lewis makes a point of clarifying the fact that communication between Thulcandra and "Deep Heaven" (where Maleldil and the eldila live) is not completely closed off. Before Ransom leaves, the Oyarsa of Malacandra tells him... "From what you have told me, I begin to see that there are eldila who go down into your air, into the very stronghold of the Bent One (Satan); your world is not so fast shut as was thought in these parts of Heaven."[31] This opens the door in the second book of the trilogy, *Perelandra*, to Ransom's learning that the Angel of the Annunciation was in fact an eldil from Deep Heaven.

In *Out of the Silent Planet*, Lewis wants to re-open peoples' imaginations to accept the possibility that other levels of reality exist beyond which we experience as strictly earthly realities. Ransom speaks of the need to do this when he says to the character (Lewis) who has recounted for the reader the events of his space journey:

> ... what we need for the moment is not so much a body of belief as a body of people familiarized with certain ideas. If we could even effect in one per cent of our readers a change-over from the conception of Space to the conception of Heaven, we should have made a beginning.[32]

This is the aim of all of Lewis's fiction: to introduce this change-over into the human imagination which will allow that imagination to break out of the constrictions imposed upon it by original sin and its effects on the human person. Sin finds expression in a power-hungry and pleasure-seeking society, which constrains the human spirit to be in awe of itself and nothing else, thereby precluding any openness to "the other" and ultimately to the Supernatural. A commentator on Lewis's fiction speaks of this need which Lewis senses to "reintroduce into human imagination the long-lost notion of blissful otherness, so much a part of the substance of myth."[33] The same author, Thomas Howard, continues:

> Perhaps one way of saying what Lewis' achievement is in *Out of the Silent Planet* would be to say that he has pressed the genre "space fiction" into the service of ancient mythic and poetic themes — so much so that the designation space fiction no longer really applies very well, since at least part of what has occurred in the drama has been the waking up, from its merely scientific torpor, of our notion of what space is. The shift from space to Deep Heaven, though, is itself only in the service of a higher theme, which is, surely, that there is a Story afoot in all worlds, and that to escape from the silence of our own world into the clarity and luminescence of another may be to find ourselves suddenly face to face with our own story, only in a clearer light and with starker colors.[34]

In *Perelandra*, the second book of "The Space Trilogy," we come upon a parallel type of a character from "our own story, only in a clearer light and with starker colors." This character is Tinidril, and she could be considered as the Perelandrian parallel to the Blessed Virgin Mary.

2. The Concept of Obedience In *Perelandra*

Bishop Robert F. Morneau, an auxiliary bishop of the Diocese of Green Bay in Wisconsin, is a noted spiritual author and lecturer in the United States. In a series of talks given at the Theology Institute of St. Norbert College in DePere, Wisconsin in the summer of 1985, he makes this comment in a lecture devoted to the life and influence of C. S. Lewis: "C. S. Lewis also wrote a trilogy on space fiction which is all theology ... a very strong theology of Mary (can be found) in one of the three volumes ..."[35] The Bishop is speaking, of course, about the second volume, *Perelandra*. This story is built upon the conceptions of reality established in the first volume and is a continuation of the first story.

As *Perelandra* begins, we find Ransom preparing for another fantastic voyage. Ransom tells the narrator of the story, Lewis himself, that he has been called to go, ultimately by Maleldil (God) Himself, to Perelandra because the Oyarsa of Thulcandra (earth) is planning an attack on Perelandra. Initially, Ransom does not know what purpose he will serve once he arrives in Perelandra, but his mission will be made known to him in time. Lewis has been selected to seal Ransom in his coffin-like spaceship and to be on hand to let him out when he returns — all the result of a chance gesture of goodness performed by Lewis who stopped by Ransom's cottage that day because of a promise he had made to do so. This small gesture of goodness lands Lewis into the center of this great plan for the salvation of Perelandra — Lewis's way of saying that the great deeds of God are often accomplished by way of the unremarkable good deeds performed by "ordinary" people. Similarly, as previously noted, Lewis is able to say of Mary, "All salvation depends on the decision which she made in the words *ecce ancilla*."[36] And so, by the power of the Oyarsa of Malacandra, Ransom is transported to Perelandra, which is out in space, but separated from Thulcandra, which has departed from the planetary "Dance of Being" due to sin. Maintaining its participation in this dance with all the other planets, Perelandra is somehow more firmly situated in "Deep Heaven," where Maleldil lives. Although far away, we shall see that the drama to be played out in Perelandra is more a reflection of the drama of earthly human life than one would imagine in reading what is often misinterpreted as mere science fiction. In fact, the experiences related by the protagonists of the "good" in this novel are explained precisely as being more vivid and more realistic than ordinary human experience. Again, the category that Lewis is utilizing here is an attempt to show that "the world beyond the world" (and the Supernature that lies within and behind nature) is more real than the ordinary human experience of things. Lewis illustrates this point in the following way: in order to understand "eldils" as "real," he points out that the distinction between the "scientific" and the "Supernatural" must disappear altogether because here we are dealing with creatures which are not animals, but which manifest themselves in "some kind of material vehicle." Lewis writes:

> The truth was that all I heard about them (eldils) served to connect two things which one's mind tends to keep separate, and that connecting gave one a sort of shock. We tend to think about nonhuman intelligences in two distinct categories which we label "scientific" and "supernatural" respectively. We think, in one mood, of Mr. Wells' Martians (very unlike the real Malacandrians, by the bye), or his Selenites. In quite a different mood we let our minds loose on the possibility of angels, ghosts, fairies, and the like. But the very moment we are compelled to recognize a creature in either class as *real* the distinction begins to get blurred: and when it is a creature like an eldil the distinction vanishes altogether. These things were not animals — to that extent one had to classify them with the second group; but they had some kind of material vehicles whose presence could (in principle) be scientifically verified. To that extent they belonged to the first group. The distinction between natural and supernatural, in fact, broke down; and when it had done so, one realized how great a comfort it had been — how it had eased the burden of intolerable strangeness which this universe imposes on us by dividing it into two halves and encouraging the mind never to think of both in the same context. What price we may have paid for this comfort in the way of false security and accepted confusion of thought is another matter.[37]

Lewis writes at length to describe his character's reaction to a vision of an eldil:

> Here at last was a bit of that world from beyond the world, which I had always supposed that I loved and desired, breaking through and appearing to my senses: and I didn't like it, I wanted it to go away.[38]

The evangelist Luke is somewhat more succinct in his description of Mary's reaction to the Annunciation of the Angel Gabriel: "But she was greatly troubled at what was said and pondered what sort of greeting this might be."[39] Throughout he Bible, we find the literary genre of the announcement of an angelic being to a woman regarding a marvelous birth which will take place through a special intervention of God.[40] According to the classical biblical schema of such announcements, the person's reaction is always characterized by fear and/or doubt. Although the Lucan scene of the Annunciation has been interpreted as departing from this classical schema on several points, exegete Ignace de la Potterie concludes that "Luke's narrative corresponds in grand measure" to the classical schema.[41] It would seem that Lewis's spiritually immature characters react in much the same way to the appearance of such celestial messengers. Thomas Howard poses the following question: "What sober justice to our experience is gained by having this sort of creature appear in a piece of adult fiction?"[42] Howard answers his own question by comparing the level of comfort which Ransom enjoys in the presence of such supernatural realities with the discomfort of the as-yet-uninitiated Lewis (the narrator). Ransom has already been to Malacandra and he has come to understand quite a bit about the "world beyond the world." Lewis the narrator, on the other hand, is just beginning his pilgrimage of experience of the "world beyond the world." He experiences "abject panic" which turns into "profound disturbance," while Ransom only senses his desire for the "other" and the "outer" increasing as the time approaches for his departure for Perelandra. As Howard puts it, "At least part of the drama, then, has entailed Ransom's progress from fear to desire in the presence of the bright realities, and Lewis's posture as a beginner here keeps this before us."[43]

Ransom's "pilgrimage" from fear to desire can itself be compared with the faith of the Blessed Virgin Mary as it is presented in the *Catechism of the Catholic Church*. While the *Catechism* calls the Blessed Virgin Mary the most perfect embodiment of obedience in faith, a faith which never waivered from the Annunciation to Calvary (#149), nevertheless the *Catechism* maintains that hers was a pilgrim faith, which traversed the "night" of faith in sharing Jesus' suffering and death (#165). We are presented with a dialectical vision of pure faith on pilgrimage — that is to say, admitting that continued growth and maturity is of the essence of what true faith is all about. The *Catechism* reserves a certain privilege to Mary in that her "engracement" by God is a prerequisite for the exercise of this perfect faith in existential growth (#490). Mary conceives Christ first in her heart through this faith — the faith which grounds her virginal maternity. Lewis is very much aware of the dynamic and changing character of the human person's faith on pilgrimage — and it is this reality which he tries to express in the contrast between (the character) Lewis's faith and the more mature faith of Ransom. Mary is the most perfect realization of such growth in faith — her pilgrimage being unique in the history of humankind because of the Immaculate Conception, or her privileged "engracement" by God. Yet she remains the model for everyone else's pilgrimage!

Let us return to the story in *Perelandra*, which is Ransom's account to Lewis and others of life on this planet. In relating the story of this place, Ransom has a difficult time expressing to his listeners the perfection of life on Perelandra as compared with life on earth. Perelandra's perfections are not a contradiction of such human realities as food and sex. Rather, on Perelandra, these realities are different because they are somehow brighter and more perfect than their earthly counterparts. Lewis's character recalls a conversation with Ransom in which a certain friend named McPhee was arguing against the Christian doctrine of the resurrection of the body. He poses the following question: " 'So you think you're going to have guts and palate forever in a world where there'll be no eating, and genital organs in a world without copulation? Man, ye'll have a grand time of it!' "[44] Ransom responds, " 'Oh, don't you see, you ass, that there's a difference between a trans-sensuous life and a non-sensuous life?' "[45] Similar to resurrection life in Heaven, life on Perelandra does not entail the death of the senses, but what we would consider a transformation of the senses as we know them. Then the magnificent tale begins.

As noted earlier, Ransom is not aware of the purpose of his mission in being sent to Perelandra. This purpose only slowly reveals itself as the drama unfolds. Arriving by spaceship, Ransom immediately experiences the novelty of Perelandra's floating islands. It seems that some of the planet's land mass floats on waves of the sea, while other land is "fixed" or stationary. He also experiences a new kind of hunger and thirst which is satisfied by the fruit of the islands in such a tremendously fulfilling fashion that no desire to repeat the satiating pleasure is felt. The "floating islands" and the lack of desire to repeat pleasures are two very significant and revelatory elements of life on Perelandra. The undulating islands will be understood by Ransom to signify the essential "fluidity" of life's experiences on Perelandra. In other words, the inhabitants of Perelandra do not find security in staking out private property which they can call their own. Rather, they are to go through life — even physically speaking — riding on the waves of Maleldil's will for them, which is continuously rolling in their direction. I think we can take this to be a reference to what life in the Garden of Eden would be like if Eden were on Perelandra and a "fall" had not occurred and the right to private property and the duty to work the land were not imposed by the Creator. Humankind would not have to stake out its territory or provide for its future because it would be living in harmony with all other creatures and Maleldil would be its sole provider. Hence there would not be present to the human mind and will the constant desire to repeat various pleasures, because the Creator could be counted upon to provide for all measure of happiness and contentment. Learning these lessons, Ransom comes to realize something very significant about human desire in its relation to God in the originally intended fashion:

> This itch to have things over again, as if life were a film that could be unrolled twice or even made to work backwards ... was it possibly the root of all evil? No: of

course the love of money was called that. But money itself — perhaps one valued it chiefly as a defence against chance, a security for being able to have things over again, a means of arresting the unrolling of the film.[46]

Humankind, in its pre-lapsarian state, could thus be understood as freely accepting the circumstances of everyday existence as they unfold in a person's life — accepting the will of God as one would accept the unfolding of a drama written by the perfect author. "Chance" would not be a threat to such existence since the creature would have perfect confidence in the author's or creator's plan for its life.

It is appropriate that soon after coming to these insights, Ransom encounters for the first time that character of Lewis's novel who is central to our thematic: the "Green Lady," who later comes to be identified as "Tinidril." Tinidril is one of the two humanoid inhabitants of Perelandra; we meet the masculine figure "Tor" at the end of the story. They are to be King and Queen of Perelandra and the parents of all its future inhabitants. Once again, Tinidril and Tor are human-like persons — not humans — extraterrestrial from our point of view.

And so Ransom has found himself in a type of paradise — Eden before the fall with Adam and Eve present — only this time on a different planet. Howard writes:

> Here he (Ransom) is in this realm of perfect harmony, and all will appear to be well: the warm climate is perfect, the fruit of the land seems inexhaustible and more than satisfying to a man's hunger, and he has a small golden-scaled dragon for a sort of mascot.[47]

The "Eve" of Perelandra identifies herself to Ransom as the "Mother." When Ransom asks her about her own mother, she replies, "looking full at him with eyes of untroubled wonder ... 'What do you mean? I *am* the Mother.'"[48] Neither of the two were embarrassed by the fact that both were entirely naked. Nor was there any arousal of sexual desire. Lewis relates Ransom's description of her:

> There was no category in the terrestrial mind which would fit her. Opposites met in her and were fused in a fashion for which we have no images. One way of putting it would be to say that neither our sacred nor our profane art could make her portrait. Beautiful, naked, shameless, young — she was obviously a goddess: but then the face, the face so calm that it escaped insipidity by the very concentration of its mildness, the face that was like the sudden coldness and stillness of a church when we enter it from a hot street — that made her a Madonna. The alert, inner silence which looked out from those eyes overawed him; yet at any moment she might laugh like a child, or run like Artemis or dance like a Maenad.[49]

While the Green Lady at first prompts the reader to a reminiscence of Eve — the first mother of earth's humanity — the words which Lewis soon puts into her mouth are unmistakably those of the new Eve — the Mother of the new creation — the Blessed Virgin Mary. Describing her position before Maleldil, the Green Lady says to Ransom:

> Only my spirit praises Maleldil who comes down from Deep Heaven into this lowness and will make me to be blessed by all the times that are rolling towards us. It is He who is strong and makes me strong and fills empty worlds with good creatures.[50]

It is obvious from the preceding paraphrase of Luke 1:46ff — the *Magnificat* — that Lewis is here invoking echoes of Mary's "Song of Praise."

When the Green Lady (Tinidril) remembers that Ransom is only one of many humans now alive on Thulcandra — since it is an older world than her own — she also realizes that therefore Ransom is not a "King," but that he is in fact an offspring from a human mother. She says to him about humans on Thulcandra, "But there are children of children of children by now, and you perhaps are one of these."[51] And so she asks Ransom to greet, on her behalf, Thulcandra's "Lady and Mother." Preserving the analogy, we perceive Thulcandra's "Lady and Mother" to be Eve, the first human woman on that planet. Ransom verifies this by responding, "Our Mother and Lady is dead."[52] And so it is clear that Lewis would have the reader parallel Tinidril with Eve as the first mothers of life on Perelandra and Thulcandra. But why does he then put the words of the *Magnificat* in Tinidril's mouth? Lewis paints a picture of Tinidril whose present existence is pre-lapsarian, and by the utilization of the words of the *Magnificat*, he parallels her with that mother — Mary — chosen by God to take the place of the first Eve in becoming a "Second Eve," a new mother of all the living! As Mary was preserved from sin from the moment of her own conception — owing to the future merits of her Divine Son — so Tinidril lives in a state free from sin according to Maleldil's plan for life on Perelandra, which has been preserved from the influence of human sin on Thulcandra.

Now Lewis would not explicitly accept an understanding of Mary as the Immaculate Conception because he would not find it to be scripturally based. In a 1945 letter to H. Lyman Stebbins, Lewis writes, "The Roman Church where it differs from this universal tradition and specially from apostolic Christianity I reject. Thus their theology about the B.V.M. I reject because it seems utterly foreign to the New Testament ..."[53] A commentator writes that Lewis's objection to Roman Catholicism "was the ordinary Protestant one, that of addition of doctrines not in the Bible, such as transubstantiation, the immaculate conception, worship of the Blessed Virgin, and papal infallibility."[54] It is not a question, for Lewis, of equating Tinidril's personal preservation from original sin with the similar preservation in Mary. In fact, Tinidril — being the first humanoid woman on Perelandra — was not immaculately conceived, but immaculately created. It is Perelandra itself and life on Perelandra as a whole that has been preserved from the influence of sin emanating from Thulcandra and its human inhabitants like Weston. And so once again, while we do not have direct allegorical equivalence between Tinidril and Mary, we do have quite overt reference to such themes as preservation from sin in the imagination of C. S. Lewis. Christopher Derrick makes this point quite well:

> ... so far as his emotions were concerned, his (Lewis's) primary response to the Church of Rome, during the last and most famous twenty years of his life was, I believe, a response of embarrassment. It confused him, he wanted it not to be there; and he was embarrassed and irritated by any reminder, arising in conversation or controversy *or in the natural logic of any fictional sequence which he was writing, that it was there, tiresomely and inescapably.*[55] (emphasis mine)

In any event, we may conclude that, since Tinidril is not a human being but a human-like creature, Lewis's story does not contradict the dogma of Mary's Immaculate Conception.

We have written at length about Lewis's anagogical style and the way in which he wanted much of his literary fiction to be interpreted. While he wanted *The Pilgrim's Regress* to be understood allegorically, he did not want this to be the case for the *Chronicles of Narnia* or "The Space Trilogy." Hence we do not see in Tinidril the allegorical figure for the Blessed Virgin Mary. But we do understand, anagogically, that the attitude of Tinidril is equivalent to the attitude of Mary. Tinidril is not a direct allegorical reference to Mary, but the equation of the two figures is certainly perceived along the lines of the Eve-Tinidril parallel and the earlier (according to Lewis's fictional chronology) Eve-Mary parallel. Tinidril is like Eve in being the first mother for a planet, but unlike Eve in that, in the end, she does not disobey Maleldil. Mary is like Eve in that she is the mother of a new creation, but unlike Eve in that she does not disobey God. Therefore, in a roundabout fashion, Tinidril is like Mary. Their attitudes are the same: characterized by obedience, openness, and receptivity to the will of the Creator. In fact, the central characteristic of the Marian attitude in *Perelandra* is obedience.

Tinidril informs Ransom that one grows old on Perelandra inasmuch as one learns some new bit of knowledge. Maturity is equated with wisdom, not with the passage of time — as it is so often characterized by earthly standards. As a result of the fall, Ransom and all earthly human beings live in "ethical time" because the human will has divorced itself from the Divine will, thereby creating the kind of "time" we know — time to choose between good and evil. On Perelandra, where humanity has not learned about the option for evil, there is no such "time" by which life spans are measured. There is only growth in accord with the will of Maleldil. The standard for all measurement is Maleldil, not matter. And so "time," if you will, is measured by the waves which undulate beneath the floating islands — waves which carry the will of Maleldil into the lives of Tinidril and Tor, who naturally accept what the Creator sends their way.

To highlight this difference between the two worlds, Lewis constructs the following dialogue between Ransom and Tinidril. Ransom begins, "But in our world not all events are pleasing or welcome. There may be such a thing that you would cut off both your arms and your legs to prevent it happening — and yet it happens: with us."[56] Tinidril responds, "But how can one wish any of those waves not to reach us which Maleldil is rolling towards us?"[57] The will of creatures on Perelandra is in perfect accord with the will of Maleldil, and this results in perfect happiness. As a result, Tinidril does not at all "know" the human fear of death or how it could be considered as something horrible because she has experienced neither fear nor horror nor anything of the sort. She finds her peace in Maleldil's will.

Then all of a sudden, Ransom begins to notice a change in her peaceful demeanor, because by his sharing with her his experience of the fear of death — "It is horrible. It has a foul smell. Maleldil himself wept when He saw it"[58] — he is forcing her to "grow older more quickly than (she) can bear."[59] This disturbance in her demeanor suggests to Ransom that even though she obediently lives out the will of Maleldil in her life, she does not do so by constraint. Her peace is not forced upon her, because here, right before Ransom's eyes, was an obvious encroachment on that peace caused by the conversation itself. She must surely be capable of an element of choice, or else she would not have experienced this moment of consternation which has resulted from her decision to listen to Ransom. In a moment of profound insight into the paradox between the sovereignty of God's will and the reality of human freedom, Ransom comes to this realization:

> It was suddenly borne in upon him that her purity and peace were not, as they had seemed, things settled and inevitable like the purity and peace of an animal — that they were alive and therefore breakable, a balance maintained by a mind and therefore, at least in theory, able to be lost. There is no reason why a man on a smooth road should lose his balance on a bicycle; but he could. There was no reason why she should step out of her happiness into the psychology of our own race; but neither was there any wall between to prevent her doing so. The sense of precariousness terrified him: but when she looked at him again he changed that word to Adventure, and then all words died out of his mind. Once more he could not look steadily at her. He knew now what the old painters were trying to represent when they invented the halo. Gaiety and gravity together, a splendour as of martyrdom yet with no pain in it at all, seemed to pour from her countenance.[60]

We have arrived at a critical point in the narrative, for it is here that Tinidril explains for Ransom and the reader what it is like to be always in perfect accord with Maleldil's will and yet remain a free creature:

> I have been so young till this moment that all my life now seems to have been a kind of sleep. I have thought that I was being carried (in the will of Maleldil), and behold, I was walking.
> ... One goes into the forest to pick food and already the thought of one fruit rather than another has grown up in one's mind. Then, it may be, one finds a different fruit and not the fruit one thought of. One joy was expected and another is given. But this I had never noticed before — that the very moment of the finding there is in the mind a kind of thrusting back or setting aside. The picture of the fruit you have *not* found is still, for a moment, before you. And if you wished — if it were possible to wish — you could keep it there. You could send your soul after the good you had expected, instead of turning it to the good you had got. You could refuse the real good; you could make the real fruit taste insipid by thinking of the other.[61]

Tinidril realizes that due to the fact that Maleldil has created her as an independent creature distinct from Himself, there must be an essential element of freedom which constitutes her very being and which enables her to construct, together with Maleldil, her own destiny — day by day! She says so beautifully:

> I thought ... that I was carried in the will of Him I love, but now I see that I walk with it. I thought that the good things he sent me drew me into them as the waves lift the islands; but now I see that it is I who plunge into them with my own legs and arms, as when we go swimming. I feel as if I were living in that roofless world of yours where men walk undefended beneath naked heaven. It is a delight with terror in it! One's own self to be walking from one good to another, walking beside Him as Himself may walk, not even holding hands. How has He made me so separate from Himself? How did it enter His mind to conceive such a thing? The world is so much larger than I thought. I thought we went along paths — but it seems there are no paths. The going itself is the path.[62]

"The going itself is the path." Lewis has so magnificently presented, within the realm of myth, the Christian belief that there is no such thing as pre-destination or a pre-determined path for human lives. Lewis shows how human beings are essentially free to create their own destinies, and that any choice against God's will constitutes slavery to sin because it carries the fear of death as a consequence. Human beings like Ransom on Thulcandra (earth) experience the fear of death because they have freely opted to choose against Maleldil's will. But this knowledge of the possibility to choose against Maleldil's will has spread neither to Malacandra nor Perelandra, whose inhabitants still enjoy that true freedom which comes with a total surrender to the will of Maleldil. Like the Immaculate Conception, they have been preserved from slavery to sin. In *Out of the Silent Planet*, the Oyarsa speaks to the evil Weston:

> Many thousands of thousand years before this, when nothing yet lived on your world, the cold death was coming on my *harandra* (high ground). Then I was in deep trouble, not chiefly for the death of my *hnau* (living

> creatures) — Maleldil does not make them long-livers — but for the things which the lord of your world, who was not yet bound, put into their minds. He would have made them as your people are now — wise enough to see the death of their kinds approaching but not wise enough to endure it. Bent counsels would soon have risen among them. They were well able to have made skyships. By me Maleldil stopped them.
>
> ... one thing we left behind us on the *harandra*: fear. And with fear, murder and rebellion. The weakest of my people does not fear death. It is the Bent One, the lord of your world, who wastes your lives and befouls them with flying from what you know will overtake you in the end. If you were subjects of Maleldil you would have peace.[63]

The obedient subject of Maleldil does not know and has not experienced sin. Without such knowledge or experience, he enjoys the true freedom of being a child of Maleldil (God) and not a slave to the Bent One (Satan).

Such is the situation of Tinidril, having been preserved from the knowledge of sin, and therefore fearless before the will of Maleldil in her life. Ransom asks her, "And have you no fear ... that it will ever be hard to turn your heart from the thing you wanted to the thing Maleldil sends?"[64] Not aware of the option to "take the easy way out" when confronted with difficult life situations, she tells Ransom that using all of your force to swim into a strong wave which Maleldil sends your way is indeed "part of the delight."[65] She adds, "How could there be anything (from Maleldil) I did not want?"[66] If Perelandra is a newer planet than Thulcandra, then Tinidril is indeed a "new Eve." Having been preserved from the counsels of the Bent One, she is equivalent to the Immaculate Conception. She has a "Marian attitude," which consists in free obedience to the will of God.

Lewis has written *Perelandra* to help the reader to "anagogically" understand how things can and did go wrong at the beginning of the human race, regardless of the way the story is told — on earth, on Perelandra, with a serpent, or with Weston. In a commentary on another Lewis story on sin and salvation, Thomas Howard writes:

> There is really no such thing as making up a wholly new story in any event: we are told that there are only ten or a dozen possible plots in the whole world. Every narrative presents some variation on those few, basic patterns.[67]

And again:

> Told in various ways, of course, this is the theme of virtually all tales of what went wrong at the beginning of the race; and this fissure between what is and what we think we might prefer lies across all drama, poetry, myth, and fiction because it lies across our experience.[68]

This, then, is what Lewis wants us to be able to get in touch with by reading his fiction: real human experience. As Howard writes, "The myths, for all their paraphernalia of gods and groves and wonders, are perhaps the truest stories ever told."[69] Once again, Tinidril is a "new Eve" and, as such, she has a "Marian attitude." She was created free from sin and her will has been preserved from the corruption of sin. Knowing that she wills not to depart from Maleldil's will, Weston's strategy is to tempt Tinidril to walk out of her own will — out of her deepest will — which is, of course, to obey Maleldil.[70] Using such word and mind games, Weston tells her that such is really the will of Maleldil for her — the ability to walk out of one's own deepest will having been left "only (for) the great."[71] Ransom brings truth to the conversation and clarity for the mind of Tinidril when he says:

> All this that we are now talking has been talked before. The thing he wants you to try has been tried before. Long ago, when our world began, there was only one man and one woman in it, as you and the King are in this. And there once before he stood, as he stands now, talking to the woman. He had found her alone as he has found you alone. And she listened, and did the thing Maleldil had forbidden her to do. But no joy and splendour came of it. What came of it I cannot tell you because you have no image of it in your mind. But all love was troubled and made cold, and Maleldil's voice became hard to hear so that wisdom grew little among

them; and the woman was against the man and the mother against the child; and when they looked to eat there was no fruit on their trees, and hunting for food took all their time, so that their life became narrower, not wider.[72]

Tinidril's deepest will, as it is described in this story, is to obey Maleldil. Lewis loves obedience to the will of God. It characterizes the perfection of every state of human life. It *is* the Marian attitude! And it is an obedience, moreover, which has as its prerequisite a participation in the obedience of Christ. The human person's obedient "yes" to the will of God in life (like Mary's *fiat*) is made possible only by the actualization of one's baptismal consecration — that is, insertion into the life of Christ. Having come to share in divine life at Baptism, the human person is only then fully capable of an obedient response to the initiatives of God. The baptized have been re-created in Christ who is the first-born of the new creation; Jesus, the second Adam, is as different (and *more* so, because He is a *divine* redeemer) from unredeemed humanity as Tor of Perelandra is different from humans of earth. And as it is in view of the merits of Christ that Mary has been, as it were, pre-inserted into the life of her Son thereby enabling her obedient response in faith, so too is this shown to be the case for Tinidril whose own obedience is, in the end, made possible by the decision of Ransom to become physically involved in her struggle against temptation by actually killing Weston after a long and tedious hand-to-hand struggle.

The parallel here is that Jesus Christ, through His incarnation, passion, death, and resurrection has become our "ransom" and by His victorious destruction of sin and death has enabled the Blessed Virgin Mary and all the baptized to hold fast to God's will in a world so filled with temptation to evil. The obedient "yes" of Mary at the Annunciation — owing as it did to the salvific work of Christ her Son — finds its parallel in the obedience of Tinidril. Thus even in the deeds of Ransom on behalf of the salvation of the inhabitants of Perelandra do we find parallels to the salvific work of Christ on behalf of the human race — that work from which the Blessed Virgin Mary benefitted and in which she took active participation.

Besides *Perelandra*, we do find other examples of the Marian attitude in the fiction of C. S. Lewis. These other examples, however, are never as comprehensive a Marian image as we find in Tinidril. We could point, for example, to Lucy in the *Chronicles of Narnia* who is the first to discover the wonderland beyond the wardrobe and the first to see Aslan. Howard calls this the "gift of recognition" when he points out that "If we read far enough in Lewis we will find a theme, hinted at in this small beginning in Narnia, of womanhood as being especially receptive to the approaches of mystery or glory, or the divine, say."[73] Howard goes on to point out Lewis's sure familiarity with "another story" wherein a woman (Mary) is invited to respond to the approaches of God: "Her flesh and indeed her very womanhood seemed to be the type and image of all human life as that life stands over against the divine life."[74] Then again, in the grand re-telling of the ancient myth of Cupid and Psyche, it is the female character Psyche in Lewis's *Till We Have Faces* who comes into direct, physical contact with the god on the mountain. Marian imagery is interspersed throughout the themes and characters of Lewis's tale. In Psyche's sister Orual, we see the slow and painful transformation of her "ugly" nature into something glorious as hinting at the bringing to birth of divinity from the womb of the lowly virgin handmaid — the theme of that "other story." These Mariological references are, however, less direct and we get the simplest and clearest portrait of the Marian attitude from Tinidril in *Perelandra*.

---

1. C. S. Lewis, *Surprised by Joy*, p. 6.

2. Ibid., pp. 10-11.

3. Ibid., p. 11.

4. Ibid.

5. Ibid.

6. Ibid., p. 10.

7. Ibid., p. 35.

8. Ibid., p. 41.

9. Ibid.

10. Ibid., p. 43.

11. Ibid., p. 66.

12. Ibid., p. 80.

13. Ibid., p. 87.

14. Ibid., pp. 93-4.

15. Ibid., p. 100.

16. Ibid., p. 110.

17. Ibid., p. 115.

18. Ibid., p. 121.

19. Ibid., pp. 121-2.

20. Ibid., p. 124.

21. Ibid., p. 125.

22. Ibid., p. 129.

23. C. S. Lewis, *Reflections on the Psalms*. (New York: Inspirational Press, 1994), p. 135.

24. _____, *Miracles*. (New York: Macmillan Publishing Company, 1947), pp. 46-7.

25. _____, "The Grand Miracle," p. 87.

26. Ibid., p. 84.

27. _____, "Priestesses in the Church?" in *God in the Dock*, pp. 235-6.

28. Cf. Chapter One, note #25.

29. C. S. Lewis, *Out of the Silent Planet*. (New York: The Macmillan Company, 1945), p. 110.

30. Ibid., p. 155.

31. Ibid.

32. Ibid., p. 167.

33. Thomas Howard, *C. S. Lewis — Man of Letters*. (San Francisco: Ignatius Press, 1987), pp. 107-8.

34. Ibid., p. 115.

35. Robert F. Morneau, "The Impact of Divine Love," an eight tape cassette series. (New York: Alba House, 1990), tape #5.

36. Cf. Chapter One, note #16.

37. C. S. Lewis, *Perelandra*. (New York: The Macmillan Company, 1944), p. 11.

38. Ibid., p. 19.

39. Luke 1:29.

40. Genesis 18:9-15. Sarah will be the mother of Isaac.
    Judges 13:2-7. Manoah's wife will be the mother of Samson.
    Luke 1:11-22. Elizabeth will be the mother of John.

41. de la Potterie, p. 7.

42. Howard, p. 130.

43. Ibid., p. 133.

44. C. S. Lewis, *Perelandra*, p. 32.

45. Ibid.

46. Ibid., p. 48.

47. Howard, p. 136.

48. C. S. Lewis, *Perelandra*, p. 66.

49. Ibid., p. 64.

50. Ibid., p. 66.

51. Ibid., p. 67.

52. Ibid.

53. Quoted from a personal letter written by Lewis in the possession of Christopher Derrick in his book, *C. S. Lewis and the Church of Rome*. (San Francisco: Ignatius Press, 1981), p. 96.

54. Clyde S. Kilby, *The Christian World of C. S. Lewis*. (Abingdon, Berks. : Markham Manor Press, 1965), p. 25.

55. Derrick, p. 56.

56. C. S. Lewis, *Perelandra*, pp. 67-8.

57. Ibid., p. 68.

58. Ibid., p. 67.

59. Ibid., p. 68.

60. Ibid.

61. Ibid., pp. 68-9.

62. Ibid., pp. 69-70.

63. C. S. Lewis, *Out of the Silent Planet*, pp. 151-2.

64. C. S. Lewis, *Perelandra*, p. 70.

65. Ibid.

66. Ibid.

67. Howard, pp. 207-8.

68. Ibid., p. 212.

69. Ibid.

70. C. S. Lewis, *Perelandra*, p. 119.

71. Ibid.

72. Ibid, p. 120.

73. Howard, p. 54.

74. Ibid.

Chapter Five
The "Joy" Of The Magnificat Is The "Joy" Of C. S. Lewis

Thus far, we have maintained that the "Marian attitude" is the necessary characteristic for the Church to fulfill its mission of establishing communion with God and unity among all of God's people. This attitude is constituted by the fervent hope, desire and expectation of the ultimate fulfillment of the new covenant of intimate union with God, which has already occurred in Jesus Christ. It is also characterized by a subsequent openness and receptivity to the Word and will of God the Father manifested by profound obedience, from the deepest will of the human person, to the will of God as it is expressed in divine revelation as well as in the believer's daily life. The Lucan *Magnificat* (Luke 1:46-55) reflects all the essential truths of the relationship between God and the Blessed Virgin Mary, and it is only in the context of that relationship with the God of Love that Mary discovers her true vocation as *Theotokos*: God-bearer. We have established that, through the continuity of the Old and New Testament Scriptures, the desire of all of Israel for salvation has come to reside powerfully in Mary and Mary's joy in that salvation reaches a crescendo in the *Magnificat* — the Canticle of Mary. Joy in the salvific nearness of Yahweh is another constitutive element of the Marian attitude, as it is also a constitutive element in the theology and life's experience of C. S. Lewis — an element which he considers necessary for Christian holiness. We will proceed to examine the profound equivalence between the joy of the *Magnificat* and the joy thematic in the works of C. S. Lewis.

A. Marian Joy In The Magnificat

And Mary said:

> *"My soul magnifies the Lord, and my spirit rejoices in God my Savior, for he has looked for favor on the lowliness of his servant. Surely, from now on all generations will call me blessed, for the Mighty One has done great things for me, and holy is his name. His mercy is for those who fear him from generation to generation. He has shown strength with his arm; he has scattered the proud in the thoughts of their hearts. He has brought down the powerful from their thrones, and lifted up the lowly. He has filled the hungry with good things, and sent the rich away empty. He has helped his servant Israel, in remembrance of his mercy, according to the promise he made to our ancestors, to Abraham and to his descendants forever." And Mary remained with her about three months and then returned to her home.*
> (Luke 1:46-56)

We shall see that modern exegetical scholarship is unanimous on the theme that the *Magnificat* is Mary's song of joy and praise on behalf of all of Israel for the wonders that God has accomplished for His daughter Zion — for Mary and for the entire nation. It stands in the Lucan gospel as Mary's response to the praise she receives from her cousin Elizabeth. Mary deflects all such praise from herself and onto Yahweh, the theme of the *Magnificat* being that all glory is due to God. The disagreement surrounding the interpretation of the *Magnificat* is centered on its origin. John McHugh summarizes the three most basic theories:

> The most ancient is that it is a canticle composed by Mary herself, probably on the occasion of her visit to Elizabeth. Another theory, of relatively modern origin, is that it is a canticle written by St. Luke and placed on Mary's lips to show forth her gratitude and humility at the honour she had received. Yet a third theory, which is fairly generally accepted nowadays, is that Luke took over, and possibly adapted, a previous composition. This third theory appears in various forms, but by far the most attractive suggestion is that the Magnificat was a hymn celebrating God's redemption of 'the lowly' and 'the poor,' composed in the early Jewish-Christian Church and later applied to Mary by the insertion of v. 48.[1]

No matter what the origin, the *Magnificat* is clearly meant to be Mary's expression of joy and gratitude over her virginal conception of the long-awaited Messiah. Echoing earlier songs of praise from the Old Testament Book of Psalms (Psalms 34, 35, 40, 70, 95, 98, 103, 104, 105) and from the canticles of other Old Testament women (Miriam, Deborah, Hannah, Judith), the *Magnificat* brings to a crescendo the sentiments of joy and thanksgiving of all of the people of Israel for a particular act of grace: "and this is the underlying assumption of the *Magnificat*: that all may join with Mary in her praise."[2] All of the emphasis is on what God has done for her and, speaking as "Daughter Zion," her joyful and praise-filled reaction to God's initiative in her life is representative of Israel's reaction to what God has accomplished on behalf of the whole nation — that is, salvation and redemption. In particular, Mary speaks for the *anawim* or the lowly ones of Israel who have long-awaited the eschatological salvation foretold throughout the Old Testament. These lowly ones are filled with joy and gladness — the classical themes of the relevant Old Testament passages which speak of the fulfillment of God's promises to Abraham and the patriarchs.[3] Bertrand Buby and Mary Catherine Nolan convey to us the sense that the *Magnificat* is primarily a joyful response to what God has already done and continues to do for Israel. Buby writes:

> Mary as a Jewish woman sings in the manner of her people praising God for his mercy and love toward her and for his strong fidelity to the covenants made with

her ancestors — Abraham and the patriarchs. Mary is self-confident and free because she centers on the power and presence of God in her own soul and memory of her people, Israel.[4]

We have earlier made reference to the work of Ignace de la Potterie, who points out that Mary "magnifies the Lord" and "rejoices in God" her Savior in response to a deed which has already been accomplished in her: namely, her having been designated by God as *kecharitomene*, a word which de la Potterie interprets as applying to one having already been transformed by the grace of God. In Mary, "the action of the grace of God has already brought about a change."[5] Nolan writes that in the *Magnificat*, "Mary, as the personification of the daughter of Zion, thus reflects the communal as well as the individual recipient of God's salvific regard."[6]

It is quite clear from a simple consideration of the basic exegetical themes of the *Magnificat* as it refers to Mary's joy that this rejoicing is not the taking of joy in herself or in her own accomplishments. It is a joy rooted totally in the grace of the "Other." Mary says, "my spirit rejoices in God my Savior" (1:47b). The writings of C. S. Lewis convey the same perspective on the true nature of Christian joy.

B. The "Joy" Of C. S. Lewis

C. S. Lewis was very much in tune with the type of joy that is to be experienced in the salvific nearness of Yahweh by means of the Incarnation of the Word and in the raising of the lowly to high places. Lewis locates joy precisely in the transformation of all of reality (except sin) into a sacrament of the presence of God. The experience of joy is the central and defining experience of Lewis's life. Lewis commentator Irene Fernandez writes:

> It should be made quite clear at the outset that this experience, which Lewis calls *joy*, is not personal in the sense of belonging to what he would refer to contemptuously as the biographical details of his life. Certainly

> it is personal to him in that he felt it with a remarkable intensity from his childhood days, but as soon as he attempted to reflect on it, he assumed that he was sharing in a common and fundamental experience of humanity.[7]

Joy is thus a fundamental human experience, according to Lewis, just as Mary's *Magnificat* was the expression of the joy of her people. And, as we have noted earlier, Lewis maintains that the human person experiences joy as a desire the fulfillment of which in our earthly experience is not greater than the desire itself. The desire through which we experience joy must therefore be rooted in a reality beyond ourselves and all of creation. It is radically experienced as a "gift." It is not a joy which is taken *in* human achievement or *in* human dignity. It is radically "Other-centered," and the "Other," of course, is ultimately God. Fernandez continues:

> For this joy is desire neither of this nor of that nor of itself, and the experience of this joy demands that one continually go beyond the objects that awaken it; in the final analysis it can only be related to an object other than all objects, an Other 'that is never fully given — nay, cannot even be imagined as given — in our present mode of subjective and spatio-temporal experience,' a 'naked Other, imageless ... unknown, undefined, desired.' This desire turns out to be the sign in us of that 'limitless demand which constitutes us,' 'the mark of the Worker on his work ...'[8]

In his written works, C. S. Lewis expresses the Marian conviction that true joy is only experienced "in God my Savior." This is the theme we will now address.

1. "My Spirit Rejoices In God My Savior"

The celebrated space trilogy concludes with *That Hideous Strength* which is so replete with hidden meaning that to categorize its characters and themes along mere allegorical lines would be to do an injustice to the depth of reality that is being expressed in this particular fictional tale. No doubt the definitive expose on the fiction of C. S. Lewis is the aforementioned *C. S. Lewis, Man of Letters*, A Reading of His Fiction by Thomas Howard. Howard exposes the layers of meaning which can be read out of much of Lewis's fiction. Howard does a particularly remarkable job in his examination of the lengthy novel, *That Hideous Strength*. Not wanting to compromise Lewis's desire that "The Space Trilogy" not be read allegorically, he only suggests that readers of *That Hideous Strength* might find a number of allusions in some of its characters to that figure in another story which we know so well — the Blessed Virgin Mary. We can say, however, that this novel is drenched in the "Marian attitude" and that it situates Christian "joy" precisely in a Marian attitude.

The story revolves around not only the marital relationship of the characters Mark and Jane, but also around the very salvation of each one, pulled as they are between the forces of good and evil. Jane, an educated and "enlightened" young woman, desires independence, self-will, and all that has to do with disassociation from the traditional roles of womanhood: wife, mother, care-giver. Nonetheless she is drawn, however reluctantly, into a community called "St. Anne's" where she is taught by its inhabitants (Ransom is the figure in charge here) that the demands of charity and truth — once heeded — will realize in a person all that it means to be human as well as bring to light for a woman the true beauty of marriage and motherhood. Accepting the teachings of those at St. Anne's, Jane ultimately becomes the salvation for her husband Mark, who conversely has been caught up in a circle of de-sensitized scientists and technocrats — de-sensitized to all that is natural or what Arthur Greeves would have called "homely" — in a group called the N.I.C.E. ("National Institute for Coordinated Experiments"). By the way, Jane's education in charity is taking shape at a place named for the mother of the Blessed Virgin Mary — a typical Lewisian allusion! Devoid of any adherence to the truth about human nature, "nice" is the only attitude for the members of the N.I.C.E. to adopt. Since there are no new stories, the evil of the N.I.C.E. is to be found in the *hubris* — or excessive pride — of its members who aim to establish a society ruled by the pure mental or spiritual power of the "Head" — a hideous creature which they attempt to keep alive separated from its body: form from matter, spirit from flesh, so that the human mind and spirit, liberated from the flesh, will ultimately be the ruling force and the end toward which all human evolution is striving.

As time goes on, it is not Mark who finds joy, but Jane who finds it in the society ruled by charity which is St. Anne's. A foreshadowing of this reality comes early in the novel when Lewis has Jane's eyes fall upon these words in a book at St. Anne's:

> The beauty of the female is the root of joy to the female as well as to the male, and it is no accident that the goddess of Love is older and stronger than the god. To desire the desiring of her own beauty is the vanity of Lilith, but to desire the enjoying of her own beauty is the obedience of Eve, and to both it is in the lover that the beloved tastes her own delightfulness. As obedience is the stairway of pleasure, so humility is the....[9]

"... it is in the lover that the beloved tastes her own delightfulness." This is Jane's first instruction in the school which teaches that true joy is to be experienced not as a state of one's own mind but as an experience of unity with that which is "other" and "outer." What Lewis called "stabs of joy" were joy's visitations in human experience — "moments of clearest consciousness ... when we became aware of our fragmentary and phantasmal nature"[10] and when we ached for reunion with the "Other."

2. Christian Joy Is Mediated Through Nature

In the *Magnificat*, Mary's words "my spirit rejoices in God my Savior" reflect the reality that true joy is found in relationship with God, "the Mighty One (who) has done great things for me." This relationship is radically effected in the Incarnation which results from the faith-filled obedience of the Blessed Virgin Mary. Howard equates the nature of receptivity or openness to the Word of God as it manifests itself in the world with the feminine aspect of reality which is portrayed in Lewis's fiction in the following way:

> This capacity which exhibits itself in these women is not an allegory for anything at all, it seems to me. Rather, it is a natural case in point of something that is hinted

> at in other stories. In the myth, it is Psyche, the soul (which in Greek is feminine), who sees the god; in another ancient story it is the woman who, unlike the prophets and patriarchs and kings who merely bear witness *to* the Word, herself bears the Word, in her womb. She has in her very anatomy a place, a home, that receives and nourishes what is true. Mere fancy, of course — but fancy that haunts the borders of myth, Gospel, and everyday biological and psychological experience.[11]

There can be no doubt that Lewis was precisely in tune with the archetypical feminine attitude — indeed, the Marian attitude — which allows the Creator to enter into deepest intimacy with His creation. Receptivity to God's initiatives toward intimacy with His creation is a feminine quality in the human person which is activated through experiences of the Divine in the world and in human experience. It is not a disembodied spirituality. It is a sensitivity to God's presence in the sacramental nature of His creation which results in what Lewis calls the "Grand Miracle" — the incarnation of the Word itself.

Thus does the Marian attitude find joy in the coincidence of apparent opposites — in the presence of the Eternal One in spatio-temporal reality. As the *Magnificat* expresses Mary's experience of God in an apparent coincidence of opposites (her lowliness will be called blessed, the powerful will be brought down while the lowly will be lifted up, the hungry will be filled and the rich will go away empty), so too is Lewis's theology filled with the discovery of joy in apparently contradictory situations. In *That Hideous Strength*, for example, it is precisely upon the lowly of the community of St. Anne that the gods shower their graces while the movers and shapers of society at the N.I.C.E., that sinister group to which Mark has been attracted, fall apart in chaotic fashion reminiscent of the fate of those who built the Old Testament Tower of Babel. Once again in Lewis's story, the "intelligentsia" of this world has been foiled while the "ordinary" has been raised on high. Howard writes:

> The mediators of these first hints of joy in Jane — in the vexed, harried, grieved Jane — are such things as

cobwebs and cigarettes and hot coffee. There is no foolishly simplistic notion here that all will be well if only we can just get a nice cup o' tea: rather, we see the whole drama proceeding in a realm where humble ordinariness is thrown into bright relief against the murky background of the abnormal and the diseased and the sophisticated.[12]

Howard locates a "coincidence of opposites" in the theology of C. S. Lewis precisely in the "Grand Miracle":

> On this accounting, it is human life that stands at the center of the whole drama. Below us there is instinctual disharmony: nature red in tooth and claw; above us there is the warfare among the principalities and powers. But somehow the locus of the business as far as we are concerned is human flesh, and this seems to be for two reasons: first, we, unlike any other creature, share both the animality of the creation below us and the rationality of the creation above us, and it is via choice that we make ourselves and hence our world either angelic or diabolical; and second, the Incarnation focused the drama forever in this human flesh. It is, somehow, a key, this flesh of ours.[13]

The "coincidence of opposites" is a theological category, medieval in origin, which we find unexplicitly utilized in the theology of C. S. Lewis.

3. "Joy" In Apparent Opposites

While Islam and, to a lesser extent, Judaism, are the religions of God's transcendence *par excellence*, and Hinduism is the religion of God's immanence, Christianity is the religion of the coincidence of the two by means of the Incarnation. The Incarnation affirms a coincidence of God and creation which neither Muslim nor Jew can accept, while the basic Christian sense of God's transcendence and the qualitative difference between God and the world, eternity and time — a tradition shared with all Semitic peoples — is foreign to the Hindu mentality. In the Incarnation, Christianity affirms a coincidence of opposites between God and creation which maintains both the continuity and the difference between Creator and creation. In a commentary on the theological thematic of the "coincidence of opposites," Ewert H. Cousins calls this thematic, which he finds present in the theology of St. Bonaventure and later in Nicholas of Cusa, a "coincidence of mutually affirming complementarity" which stresses both the unity and difference between God and His creation. Cousins writes:

> ... opposites genuinely coincide while at the same time continuing to exist as opposites. They join in a real union, but one that does not obliterate differences; rather it is precisely the union that intensifies the difference. The more intimately the opposites are united, the more they are differentiated. ... An example of this can be seen in the doctrine of the complementarity of the Ying — Yang, or the male and female principles, in Taoism. A similar complementarity is found in the Western personalistic philosophy of such thinkers like Martin Buber, who analyzes the mutuality involved in the I — Thou relation: the more one relates to the other as *Thou*, the more he becomes an *I*. The principle of complementarity becomes a cosmic principle of evolution in the thought of Teilhard de Chradin. On all levels of the universe and at all stages of the evolutionary process, Teilhard sees a single law operating — the law of creative union, which he articulates in the terse formula: union differentiates. The more a particle of matter or a human person enters into a creative union with another, the more their true uniqueness is achieved.
>
> ... I believe that Bonaventure falls squarely and consistently within this (third) class, for his thought emphasizes both unity and difference. On all levels of his vision, one finds the coincidence of mutually affirming complementarity: in the doctrine of the Trinity, creation, God's relation to the world, man as image of God, Christology, the return of the soul to God and the realization of mystical union. For example, Bonaventure maintains the Semitic affirmation of the difference of God and the world, not merely by affirming their opposition, but by affirming God's transcendence precisely through his immanence.[14]

There is a difference between the coincidence of created opposites (e.g., the "Ying-Yang" coincidence of Taoism) — known by reason — and the coincidence between Supernature and nature — known through divine revelation and accepted by faith. The latter realm includes the Incarnation. Cousins continues:

> Through grace it is possible for man to be lifted up to this realm, thus overcoming his radical difference and participating in the divine life of the Trinity made available by Christ.
> ... Bonaventure employs a Trinitarian model, in which a third element acts as mediating principle unifying the opposites. The Trinitarian model is the classical Christian model of the coincidence of opposites, for it contains both bi-polarity and a unifying mediating principle. From one point of view the Son is seen as the mediating principle between the Father and the Spirit. In each case unity and bi-polarity are affirmed by the triadic model. The Trinitarian model, with its logic of the coincidence of opposites, permeates Bonaventure's entire system ... for Bonaventure sees vestiges of the Trinity everywhere.[15]

Christ in the Incarnation is the "unifying mediating principle" between nature and Supernature and C. S. Lewis, like Bonaventure, "sees vestiges of the Trinity everywhere"! There is much more that could be said about the history and development of the theology of the coincidence of opposites, but we must now turn to where this thematic is prevalent in the writings of C. S. Lewis.

Like Mary in the *Magnificat*, Lewis locates joy in the coincidence of apparent opposites. This is a theology which can be seen to have been present in the writings of the seventeenth-century Anglican divines. Allchin sees this theology permeating their writings, with Mary as the central human character in their theological drama. He writes:

> Here already the place of Mary within the Christian dispensation is clearly coming into view. God enters into the material world. He is present at the roots of man's affective, natural, bodily life. The fullness of deity is revealed not only in the mind and speech of Jesus,

> but in his body, that which he took from us, that in which he is most at one with us. The most basic of human experiences, of needs and satisfactions, fulfillments and anxieties are the soil in which the divine is revealed and grows. Every human act, rooted in the material, animal order, for man is part of the material world and shares much with the animal creation, can yet become fully human, in becoming free and consciously realized, can indeed be known as a gift, discovered as a response of thanks to God, can be divine. Grace shines through, illuminates and transfigures the natural order in its totality, shows that it has a wholly unexpected goal and destiny; for God has entered into the very processes of birth.
>
> ... Hence everywhere in the Christian world where she is known, Mary's name is associated with joy. She is the joy of joys, the cause of our joy, the joy of all creation. Latin, Greek, Russian, Syriac all proclaim the same thing. In her there is a meeting of opposites, of God and man, of flesh and spirit, of time and eternity, which causes an explosion of joy, of a kind of ecstasy. It is the joy which is known in human life, 'when the opposites come together, and the genuinely new is born.'[16]

Lewis came to know and treasure this kind of joy in his life, as we shall now see through his writings.

Lewis found joy in the coincidence of opposites on both the natural and the supernatural level. His autobiography reveals to us the growth of his appreciation for locating truth and beauty in what Arthur Greeves taught him to call the "homely." Lewis learned from Greeves the ability to attach lasting value to simple experiences like weather, food, the family, the neighborhood. Arthur helped to develop in Lewis a particular sensitivity to the Supernatural which lay within and behind the world of nature. Here we see in Lewis the beginnings of his appreciation for the coincidence between God and creation, adding to his eventual understanding of the sacramental value of all creation. On the strictly natural level, we have quoted above the following line from Lewis's autobiography which gives a depth of meaning to his valuation of the unity of opposites. Speaking of his companionship with Arthur, he writes,

"But best of all we liked it when the homely and the unhomely met in sharp juxtaposition."[17]

In his attempts to describe his experiences of joy, Lewis talks about it as the reconciliation between desire and fulfillment. Since joy is a desire the fulfillment of which he has not yet experienced, thereby making the desire itself desirable, he writes, "... the very nature of Joy makes nonsense of our common distinction between having and wanting. There, to have is to want and to want is to have. Thus, the very moment when I longed to be so stabbed again (by joy), was itself such a stabbing."[18] Thus does Lewis come into contact with the Desirable One (the "Other": God) in particular moments of his own experience — a gift from without expressing itself within his own life. Of the sacramental value of life's experiences, Lewis writes:

> The comparison is of course between something of infinite moment and something very small; like comparison between the Sun and the Sun's reflection in a dewdrop. Indeed, in my view, very like it, for I do not think the resemblance between the Christian and the merely imaginative experience is accidental. I think that all things, in their way, reflect heavenly truth, the imagination not least. "Reflect" is the important word. This lower life of the imagination is not a beginning of, nor a step toward, the higher life of the spirit, merely an image. In me, at any rate, it contained no element either of belief or of ethics; however far pursued, it would never have made me either wiser or better. But it still had, at however many removes, the shape of the reality it reflected.[19]

Thus did Lewis learn that when moments of joy came, he did not have to break away from the sensible realities which mediated those joys, as if "to seek some bodiless light shining beyond them."[20] Rather, the light shone out of the sensible images, "transforming all common things and yet itself unchanged."[21]

The coincidence of opposites in nature and the coincidence of nature and Supernature was the "stuff" of joy for C. S. Lewis, as it was for the Blessed Virgin Mary. That God should reveal Himself in all His fullness to the lowly maiden of Nazareth, and that Mary should recognize and embrace this revelation is the ultimate realization of

Christian joy. Before coming to explicit belief in the Christian God, Lewis's musings on the "Absolute Spirit" which he had come to accept were valuable inasmuch as they compelled him to perceive that the "Absolute," the "Other," which lay behind the images was in fact a reality wherein all unity is achieved: "The Absolute was 'there,' and that 'there' contained the reconciliation of all contraries, the transcendence of all finitude, the hidden glory which was the only perfectly real thing there is."[22] Gradually, Lewis came to realize that the "Absolute" could not be made clear — he could not enjoy a personal relationship with it — unless and until he "met" God. This eventually happened, mediated through the simplest of all experiences — God reached out to C. S. Lewis on the top of a double-decker bus, going up Headington Hill. It was the high-point of a lengthy conversion experience: "I felt as if I were a man of snow beginning to melt."[23] And God came in![24] His ultimate acceptance of the Incarnation was the final step in his acceptance of a "concrete," "immanent" God. "Surprised by Joy" means, really, "Surprised by Christ." And Mary was at the ready to be the first one to embrace this surprise!

Other instances of finding God — finding joy — in a coincidence of opposites are scattered throughout Lewis's works. If unity is the principle of Christian holiness, then that which is holy must be present in the coming-together of that which is distinct, "For," as Lewis writes, "union exists only between distincts ... God created: He caused things to be other than Himself that, being distinct, they might learn to love Him, and achieve union instead of mere sameness."[25] The coincidence of opposites, or at least of distinctions, is part of the very nature of God in our Christian understanding of the Trinity, and as such, runs throughout all of created reality. Lewis writes:

> The Father eternally begets the Son and the Holy Ghost proceeds: deity introduces distinction within itself so that the union of reciprocal loves may transcend mere arithmetical unity or self-identity.
>   ... From before the foundation of the world He (the Son) surrenders begotten Deity back to begetting Deity in obedience. And as the Son glorifies the Father, so also the Father glorifies the Son.

> ... As we draw nearer to its uncreated rhythm, pain and pleasure sink almost out of sight. There is joy in the dance, but it does not exist for the sake of joy. It does not even exist for the sake of good, or of love. It is Love Himself, and Good Himself, and therefore happy. It does not exist for us, but we for it.[26]

The rhythm of "the Dance" which is the love-sharing life of the Trinity contains the reconciliation of all apparent opposites and distinctions, because it is the source of those distinctions. The world itself is described by Lewis as participating in a dance in which the good, descending from God, is disturbed by the evil arising from creatures, with the resulting conflict only being resolved by the Incarnation — God's assumption of the suffering nature which evil produces.[27] And Mary is present at the grand miracle of this coincidence between God and human nature. In the coincidence, her spirit finds joy (cf. the *Magnificat*). In an essay on the Incarnation entitled "The Grand Miracle," Lewis describes the sanctification of nature in the following way:

> ... the Christian story is precisely the story of one grand miracle, the Christian assertion being that what is beyond all space and time, what is uncreated, eternal, came into nature, into human nature, descended into His own universe, and rose again, bringing nature up with Him. It is precisely one great miracle. If you take that away there is nothing specifically Christian left.[28]

Lewis wants his readers to understand that all of nature — created reality — is not as "ordinary" as it might seem. Indeed, it is precisely in and through the ordinary that God allows His glory to shine. In his attempts to educate his nephew Wormwood in the proper technique of tempting humans to evil, the more experienced devil Screwtape advises him to keep his subject focused on the ordinary nature of ordinary things — so that the subject might not perceive the glory that is hidden in a world that has been redeemed. Screwtape advises Wormwood, "... they find it all but impossible to believe in the unfamiliar while the familiar is before their eyes. Keep pressing home on them the *ordinariness* of things."[29] As we have mentioned earlier, it was the Blessed Virgin Mary who exalted in her "ordinariness" and lowliness! The sacramental nature of all reality (except sin) demands that we not leave the world and its "ordinariness" behind in our efforts to achieve communion with God. It is not in spite of the world that we perceive the Supernatural, but precisely in the world and in human nature that we see God at work. In *The Abolition of Man*, Lewis says, "It is no use trying to 'see through' first principles. If you see through everything, then everything is transparent. But a wholly transparent world is an invisible world. To 'see through' all things is the same as not to see."[30]

Lewis would rather have us "look along" things in order to see the reality within and behind them, rather than merely "look at" things and try to figure out how God is present in them all. That would lead to pantheism. "Looking along" things would better lead us to their Origin and Creator. In the essay "Meditation in a Toolshed," Lewis talks about seeing the sun at the far end of a beam of light rather than looking "at" the beam and reasoning as to its source. There is a difference between "looking along" and "looking at." It is better to "look along" and actually see the thing emanating from its source, rather than looking at the thing itself in isolation. He explains the difference in this way:

> But this is only a very simple example of the difference between looking at and looking along. A young man meets a girl. The whole world looks different when he sees her. Her voice reminds him of something he has been trying to remember all his life, and ten minutes casual chat with her is more precious than all the favours that all other women in the world could grant. He is, as they say, 'in love.' Now comes a scientist and describes this young man's experience from the outside. For him it is all an affair of the young man's genes and a recognised biological stimulus. That is the difference between looking *along* the sexual impulse and looking *at* it.[31]

This "looking along" of human and earthly realities is really the way in which Lewis describes Mary and Joseph's acceptance of the miracle of the Virgin Birth. The coincidence of humanity and divinity in the Incarnation is a reality which finds its origin far beyond the womb of the Virgin Mary — in that original unity (God) where all lines meet and all contrasts are explained: "We catch sight of a new key principle — the power of the Higher, just insofar as it is truly Higher, to come down, the power of the greater to include the less ... Everywhere the great enters the little — its power to do so is almost the test of its greatness ... The pattern is there in nature because it was first there in God"[32] Therefore, the style of God's action in the Incarnation runs through all of redeemed nature. Of this originating power or momentum which is found in God and shared with nature, Lewis writes:

> In a normal act of generation the father has no creative function ... Behind every spermatozoon lies the whole history of the universe ... The weight or drive behind it is the momentum of the whole interlocked event which we call Nature up-to-date ... If we believe that God created Nature, that momentum comes from Him ... no woman ever conceived a child, no mare a foal, without Him (God). But once, and for a special purpose, He dispensed with that long line which is His instrument: once His life-giving finger touched a woman without passing through the ages of interlocked events. Once the great glove of Nature was taken off His hand. His naked hand touched her. There was of course a unique reason for it. That time he was creating not simply a man but the Man who was to be Himself: was creating man anew: was beginning at this divine and human point, the New Creation of all things. The whole soiled and weary universe quivered at this direct injection of essential life — direct, uncontaminated, not drained through all the crowded history of Nature.[33]

Mary's ability to accept the invitation to be the mother of the Lord came from her firm belief that God does act in the natural order — always, because all of the momentum comes from Him in the first place, and sometimes miraculously, because, believing in God as the Lord and Creator of nature, Mary understood God to be able to intervene in nature's processes at His will. This faith conviction is at the heart of Mary's joy: "My spirit rejoices in God my Savior."

Lewis would say that, although all things are *not* one, all things come from one and are thus related in varied and complicated ways.[34] God's glory thus shines through even those things which we might consider opposites — like the humanity and divinity of Christ — if we understand all of reality as emanating from the Unity which is God. Indeed, according to what seems to be God's way of acting throughout salvation history, He loves to shine through opposites: to choose the weak and make them strong, to choose a virgin and make her fruitful, to bring the most glorious life out of even the most ignominious death. For the Christian, as for Mary, joy can be found in such coincidence of opposites.

---

1. John McHugh, *The Mother of Jesus in the New Testament*. (New York: Doubleday and Company, Inc., 1975), p. 73.

2. Ibid., p. 75.

3. Mary Catherine Nolan, O. P., Mary's Song: *Canticle of a Liberated People*, doctoral dissertation (International Marian Research Institute, University of Dayton, Ohio: 1995), pp. 34 ff.

4. Bertrand Buby, S. M., *Mary, The Faithful Disciple*. (New York, Paulist Press, 1985), p. 74.

5. de la Potterie, *Mary in the Mystery of the Covenant*, p. 18.

6. Nolan, p. 34.

7. Irene Fernandez, "C. S. Lewis on Joy" in *Communio*, (Fall, 1982), p. 248.

8. Ibid., p. 251.

9. C. S. Lewis, *That Hideous Strength*. (New York: The Macmillan Company, 1946), pp. 62-3.

10. C. S. Lewis, *Surprised by Joy*, p. 121.

11. Howard, *C. S. Lewis: Man of Letters*, p. 171.

12. Ibid., pp. 184-5.

13. Ibid., pp. 190-1.

14. Ewert H. Cousins, "Bonaventure, The Coincidence of Opposites and Nicholas of Cusa" in *Studies Honoring Ignatius Charles Brady, Friar Minor*, Romano Stephen Almagno, O. F. M. and Conrad L. Harkins, O. F. M., eds. (St. Bonaventure, N. Y.: The Franciscan Institute, 1976), pp. 180-1.

15. Ibid., pp. 182-3.

16. Allchin, *The Joy of All Creation*, pp. 4-5.

17. C. S. Lewis, *Surprised by Joy*, p. 87.

18. Ibid., p. 93.

19. Ibid.

20. Ibid., p. 100.

21. Ibid.

22. Ibid., p. 115.

23. Ibid., p. 123.

24. In his autobiography, Lewis speaks of the influence of one of his students, now the well-known Dom Bede Griffiths, in his conversion experience (*Surprised by Joy*, p. 123). It is interesting to note that recently Griffiths, an Indian priest and respected theological author, has produced a video cassette interview entitled "The Necessity of the Feminine" (Sydney, Australia: MTI Films, 1993), in which he describes a powerful religious experience of the feminine aspect of reality and human life. He describes this experience in terms of the traditional theological category of the coincidence of opposites.

25. Lewis, *The Problem of Pain*, pp. 138-9.

26. Ibid., pp. 139-41.

27. Ibid., p. 72.

28. C. S. Lewis, "The Grand Miracle" in *God in the Dock*, p. 80.

29. C. S. Lewis, *The Screwtape Letters*. (New York: Macmillan Publishing Company, 1982), p. 10.

30. C. S. Lewis, *The Abolition of Man*. (New York: Macmillan Publishing Company, 1955), p. 91.

31. C. S. Lewis, "Meditation in a Toolshed" in *God in the Dock*, p. 212.

32. C. S. Lewis, *Miracles*, pp. 111-12.

33. Ibid., p. 138.

34. Ibid., p. 165.

Chapter Six
The Marian Attitude And The Christian Attitude: Lewisian Weaknesses And Strengths

In his book *Mere Christianity*, renowned for its ecumenical applications, Lewis writes as follows in the Introduction:

> Some people draw unwarranted conclusions from the fact that I never say more about the Blessed Virgin Mary than is involved in asserting the Virgin Birth of Christ. But surely my reason for not doing so is obvious? To say more would take me at once into highly controversial regions. And there is no controversy between Christians which needs to be so delicately touched as this. The Roman Catholic beliefs on that subject are held not only with the ordinary fervour that attaches to all sincere religious belief, but (very naturally) with the peculiar and, as it were, chivalrous sensibility that a man feels when the honour of his mother or his beloved is at stake. It is very difficult so to dissent from them that you will not appear to them a cad as well as a heretic. And contrariwise, the opposed Protestant beliefs on this subject call forth feelings which go down to the very roots of all Monotheism whatever. To radical Protestants it seems that the distinction between

> Creator and creature (however holy) is imperilled: that Polytheism is risen again. Hence it is hard so to dissent from them that you will not appear something worse than a heretic — an idolator, a Pagan. If any topic could be relied upon to wreck a book about "mere" Christianity — if any topic makes utterly unprofitable reading for those who do not yet believe that the Virgin's son is God — surely this is it.[1]

In this book, the question that initially and finally must be squarely faced comes from the warning that Lewis himself posed to his readers regarding his writings: are we drawing unwarranted and unsubstantiated conclusions about his attitude toward Mary? Certainly, the claims that have been made towards exposing a "Marian attitude" in the works of C. S. Lewis have not gone unsubstantiated. The substance for this claim has been laid out and evaluated in the preceding chapters. As far as the conclusions being termed "unwarranted," we may quote another paragraph from *Mere Christianity*:

> ... I should be very glad if people would not draw fanciful inferences from my silence on certain disputed matters.
>
> For example, such silence need not mean that I myself am sitting on the fence. Sometimes I am. There are questions at issue between Christians to which I do not think I have the answer. There are some to which I may never know the answer: if I had asked them, even in a better world, I might (for all I know) be answered as a far greater questioner was answered: "What is that to thee? Follow thou Me." But there are other questions as to which I am definitely on one side of the fence, and yet say nothing.[2]

Whatever has been gleaned from the writings of C. S. Lewis in the present work will hopefully be accepted as far from "fanciful inference." All claims have been substantiated by an appeal to his theological heritage and certain other strong influences on his theological mind; and, more importantly, these claims have been substantiated by the most direct references to the writings of Lewis himself. The "Marian attitude" pervades his works and constitutes a particular way of appreciating his idea of Christian discipleship. We have defined the Marian attitude in terms of hope, desire, and expectation on the part of the believer for the fulfillment of a covenant of intimate union with God. Such an attitude is characterized, of necessity, by an openness and receptivity to the Word and will of God which is manifested in profound obedience to that will. The Marian attitude is also defined by the uniquely Marian joy of the *Magnificat* — a joy which revels in the salvific nearness of Yahweh in the Incarnation and which is often found in the coincidence of created opposites as well as in the coincidence of Divinity and humanity in the womb of the Blessed Virgin. These conclusions have been drawn from five major theological themes which we have found to run uniformly through the life's experience and written works of C. S. Lewis, namely, the centrality of the Incarnation in the economy of salvation, the hierarchical ordering of all of reality, the discontinuity and continuity between Supernaturalism and naturalism, obedience, and the relation of the masculine to the feminine aspects of reality according to the Supernatural archetype of this relationship.

Our greatest concern is to not have done damage to Lewis by imposing a Mariology which is explicitly expressed in his biographical history or developed systematically in his apologetical or fictional works. Surely, C. S. Lewis did not formulate such an explicit "mariology" in his life-time. Nonetheless, his very own wish for much of his writing was that it be interpreted imaginatively or "anagogically." Such a desire on his part affirms that we do not do him harm by taking from our experience of his writings an appreciation of what can validly and profoundly be described as the "Marian attitude" of his works.

While we can appreciate the "Marian attitude" that we have seen in Lewis, it would be improper to conclude that his presentation of this attitude is exhaustive of all the richness which the Church, down through the centuries, has ascribed to the Mother of God.

For example, the uniqueness of the "Marian attitude" within the context of the general Christian attitude is not an issue with Lewis, as it is in Roman Catholic theology. Such "uniqueness" is the result of Mary's Divine maternity, that is, the honor bestowed on her as the one chosen to be the Mother of the Lord. It is for this that Elizabeth calls Mary "blest" at the Visitation (Luke 1:42), and again "blessed" because of her faith which made possible the fulfillment of God's promise. Joseph Fitzmyer writes, "Two aspects of Mary are thus praised, her motherhood of him who is *kyrios*, but above all her faith."[3] It would seem that most of Lewis's emphasis is on the example of Mary's faith — the discipleship of the one who hears the Word of God and keeps it (Luke 8:21). His emphasis therefore presents to us a "general" Marian attitude as opposed to a personal (hence more Catholic) Marian attitude wherein Mary has a unique place in the Communion of Saints — a place in which all disciples can develop a relationship with her as with a heavenly mother because she has been chosen to be such by the Lord (John 19:26-27). This is obviously a result of Lewis's emphasis (and properly so) on the centrality of the event of the Incarnation. Even though, as we have seen, Lewis recognizes the uniqueness of Mary's role in the plan of salvation, and thereby in the work of redemption, he places much less emphasis on the privileges that accompany divine maternity. His great emphasis on the model of Mary's discipleship as Mother of the Lord in the work of redemption and his shortcomings with regard to Mary's maternity of all of the members of Christ's body make Lewis, I think, neither a Marian "minimalist" nor a Marian "maximalist" but somewhere in between!

Christopher Derrick fantasizes about what a "Roman Catholic Lewis" would have been like. Obviously, this is no more than pure speculation, because Lewis never even hinted about any desire on his part for conversion from Anglicanism. Derrick speculates as follows:

> One should not pry into a man's devotional life, even when it is purely hypothetical. I may perhaps suggest, however, that as soon as a Catholic Lewis had overcome certain blocks and barriers within himself — these being cultural and psychological rather than theological in nature — he might have felt obliged to make an *amende honorable* to the Mother of Jesus and might not have stopped at that point. He did have some understanding of what this devotion means to Catholics and of the sense in which it is a natural flowering of

their faith. I can well imagine it becoming a late though vigorous flowering of his own faith.[4]

Hypothesis, speculation, and fanciful imagination — while these were all the stuff of Lewis's literary and even theological world, they have not been the basis of the present work. The present work has not been concerned with Lewis's attitude toward Marian devotion. We have not been concerned with Lewis's affection for Mary. What has indeed concerned us is precisely *Lewis's vision* of the *Christian attitude*. A friend of Lewis, Sheldon Vanauken, relates the experience of a summer-time dinner with the Oxford don. Vanauken's wife, Davy, asked Lewis about praying to Mary. Vanauken writes of Lewis's response in the following way:

> Lewis would never commit himself on anything having to do with differences between high church and low. He did say, though, that if one's time for prayer was limited, the time one took for asking Mary's help was time one might be using for going directly to the Most High.[5]

Lewis did not write about Marian devotion. He wrote about the most fundamental characteristics of the Christian life ('Mere Christianity') and he did not hesitate to attribute all of these characteristics to Mary, as we have shown by an examination of his scant but strong references to her in his writings. In the above-referenced book, Vanauken quotes a letter he received from Lewis in which Lewis addresses the couple's decision not to have children. Lewis's letter reads, in part, as follows:

> The idea behind your voluntary sterility, that an experience, e.g. maternity, which cannot be shared should on that account be avoided, is surely very unsound. For a. (forgive me) the conjugal act itself depends on opposite, reciprocal and therefore unshare-able experiences. Did you want her to feel she had a *woman* in bed with her? b. The experience of a woman denied maternity is one you *did not and could not* share with her. To be denied paternity is different, trivial in comparison.

> ... You spared her (very wrongly) the pains of childbirth: do not evade your own, the travail you must undergo while Christ is being born in you. Do you imagine she herself can now have any greater care about you than that this spiritual maternity of yours should be patiently suffered and joyfully delivered?[6]

Lewis is here referring to Vanauken's grief over the premature death of his beloved wife, calling this pain a "spiritual maternity" which must be brought to full term in obedience to God's will (i.e., it would be unwise for Vanauken to contemplate suicide as a way to be re-joined with his wife. Suicide would constitute disobedience to the will of God, while obedience was to be thought of as the highest virtue). Honoring Davy as the obedient one, Lewis writes "Disobedience is not the way to get nearer to the obedient."[7]

Lewis would not have thought in terms of obedience and spiritual maternity without having thought of the Blessed Virgin Mary. Earlier, Vanauken had sent this sonnet to Lewis, entitled *Advent*, which he had written:

> *Our Lord is suffering still — there is no end*
> *of pain: the spear pierces, nails rend —*
> *And we below with Mary weep our loss.*
>
> *The chilling edge of night crawls round the earth;*
> *At every second of the centuries*
> *The dark comes somewhere down, with dreadful ease*
> *Slaying the sun, denying light's rebirth.*
>
> *But if the agony and death go on,*
> *Our Lady's tears, Our Lord's most mortal cry,*
> *So, too, the timeless lovely birth again —*
> *And the forsaken tomb. Today: the dawn*
> *That never ended and can never die*
> *In breaking glory ushers in the slain.*[8]

For our purposes, Lewis's reply to having received this poem is important. He writes: "I think all the sonnets really good. *The Sands* is very good, indeed. So is *Advent*, perhaps it is best ..."[9] Admittedly, one can only assume that, in calling this sonnet the "best,"

Lewis did not have grave misgivings about the theology expressed in and by the poem. If this is the case, then we can safely assume Lewis's agreement with the idea that while Our Lady's tears still flow over the continuing agony of her Son, so too does she rejoice in wonder at "the timeless lovely birth again," which goes on for the members of her Son's Body — that birth to life which first entered the world through Mary and continues to be born of the Marian attitude!

Lewis loved the obedience of the Blessed Virgin Mary. As we have seen, it is a major topic of *Perelandra*, the second book of his fictional space trilogy. As we have noted time and again, Lewis's reference to Mary's *Ecce ancilla* should be understood as the quintessential human response — in obedience — to the Divine initiative in human affairs. Of this Marian attitude — this *fiat* attitude, if you will — Lewis writes:

> ... Christian society ... is always insisting on obedience — obedience (and outward marks of respect) from all of us to properly appointed magistrates, from children to parents, and (I am afraid this is going to be very unpopular) from wives to husbands.[10]

And:

> I may repeat "Do as you would be done by" till I am black in the face, but I cannot really carry it out till I love my neighbor as myself: and I cannot learn to love my neighbor as myself till I learn to love God: and I cannot learn to love God except by learning to obey Him.[11]

Obedience to the will of God does not preclude the fulfillment of the most profound human joy and satisfaction in a person's life. Indeed it is the prerequisite for such fulfillment. Intimacy with the Divine — union with God who is the source of all being — is both component part and consequence of the Marian attitude. Lewis writes:

> I think all Christians would agree with me if I said that though Christianity seems at first to be all about morality, all about duties and rules and gifts and virtue, yet it leads you on, out of all that, into something beyond. One has a glimpse of a country where they do not talk of those things, except perhaps as a joke. Every one there is filled with what we should call goodness as a mirror is filled with light.[12]

Our intimacy with the Divine comes from the grace with which God's Spirit — God's goodness or love — fills our lives as light fills a mirror.

C. S. Lewis understood that unity with God is at the heart of Christian holiness. Since this unity has been most perfectly realized in the Incarnation — the union of the Divine with the human in the God-man Jesus Christ — the Christian is able to find holiness in the world — in the flesh — by a "pilgrim's regress" through created reality, perceiving within and behind it the vast realm of uncreated Reality. With this understanding, Lewis effectively achieves his goal of baptizing the human imagination and senses — sensitizing the human person to the presence of God in the world. Mary is the human person, *par excellence*, who was attentive to this reality in the world. The attitude that characterized her earthly life, expressed in various ways (literal, allegorical, and anagogical) in the writings of C. S. Lewis, is for Lewis the quintessential Christian attitude.

---

1. C. S. Lewis, *Mere Christianity*, p. vii.

2. Ibid., pp. vi-vii.

3. Joseph A. Fitzmyer, S. J., *The Gospel According to Luke (I-IX)* in *The Anchor Bible* series. (New York: Doubleday & Company, Inc., 1981), p. 358.

4. Derrick, *C. S. Lewis and the Church of Rome*, p. 217.

5. Sheldon Vanauken, *A Severe Mercy*. (San Francisco: Harper San Francisco, 1987), p. 121.

6. Ibid., pp. 209-10.
7. Ibid., p. 210.
8. Ibid., p. 122.
9. Ibid., p. 124.
10. C. S. Lewis, *Mere Christianity*, p. 65.
11. Ibid., p. 68.
12. Ibid., p. 116.

Bibliography

A. Primary Sources: Works Of C. S. Lewis
(arranged in chronological order of publication)

THE PILGRIM'S REGRESS, An Allegorical Apology for Christianity, Reason and Romanticism. Grand Rapids, Michigan: Eerdmans, 1958 (first published in London in 1933).

THE ALLEGORY OF LOVE, A Study in Medieval Tradition. New York: Oxford University Press, 1958 (first published in London in 1936).

OUT OF THE SILENT PLANET. New York: The Macmillan Company, 1945 (first published in London in 1938).

THE PROBLEM OF PAIN. New York: The Macmillan Company, 1945 (first published in London in 1940).

THE SCREWTAPE LETTERS, with Screwtape Proposes a Toast. New York: Macmillan Publishing Company, 1982 (first published in London in 1942, with *Toast* in 1961).

THE CASE FOR CHRISTIANITY. New York: The Macmillan Company, 1943 (first published in London as *BROADCAST TALKS* in 1942).

CHRISTIAN BEHAVIOUR, A further series of Broadcast Talks. New York: The Macmillan Company, 1943.

PERELANDRA. New York: The Macmillan Company, 1944 (first published in London in 1943).

THE ABOLITION OF MAN, or Reflections on Education with Special Reference to the Teaching of English in the Upper Forms of Schools. New York: The Macmillan Company, 1947 (first published in London in 1943).

BEYOND PERSONALITY, The Christian Idea of God. New York: The Macmillan Company, 1945 (first published in London in 1944).

THAT HIDEOUS STRENGTH, A Modern Fairy-Tale for Grown-Ups. New York: The Macmillan Company, 1946 (first published in London in 1945).

THE GREAT DIVORCE, A Dream. New York: The Macmillan Company, 1946 (first published in London in 1945).

GEORGE MACDONALD, AN ANTHOLOGY: 365 Readings. C. S. Lewis, ed. New York: Simon and Schuster, 1996 (first published by Macmillan in London in 1947).

MIRACLES, A Preliminary Study. New York: The Macmillan Company, 1947.

THE WEIGHT OF GLORY AND OTHER ADDRESSES. New York: The Macmillan Company, 1949 (originally published in London as *TRANSPOSITION, and Other Addresses* in the same year).

THE LION, THE WITCH AND THE WARDROBE, A Story for Children. New York: The Macmillan Company, 1950.

PRINCE CASPIAN, The Return to Narnia. New York: The Macmillan Company, 1951.

MERE CHRISTIANITY. New York: Macmillan Publishing Company, 1960 (first published in London in 1952).

THE VOYAGE OF THE "DAWN TREADER". New York: The Macmillan Company, 1952.

THE SILVER CHAIR. New York: The Macmillan Company, 1953.

ENGLISH LITERATURE IN THE SIXTEENTH CENTURY EXCLUDING DRAMA. Oxford: Clarendon Press, 1954.

THE HORSE AND HIS BOY. New York: The Macmillan Company, 1954.

THE MAGICIAN'S NEPHEW. New York: The Macmillan Company, 1955.

SURPRISED BY JOY, The Shape of My Early Life in *The Inspirational Writings of C. S. Lewis.* New York: Inspirational Press, 1994 (first published in London in 1955).

THE LAST BATTLE. New York: The Macmillan Company, 1956 (originally published the same year in London as *THE LAST BATTLE, A Story for Children*).

TILL WE HAVE FACES, A Myth Retold. New York: Harcourt, Brace and World, 1957 (first published in London in 1956).

THE ALLEGORY OF LOVE, A Study in Medieval Tradition. New York: Oxford University Press, 1958.

REFLECTIONS ON THE PSALMS. New York: Harcourt, Brace and World, 1958.

THE FOUR LOVES. New York: Harcourt, Brace and World, 1960.

A PREFACE TO PARADISE LOST. New York: Oxford University Press, 1961.

A GRIEF OBSERVED. Greenwich, CT: Seabury Press, 1963 (under the pseudonym of N.W. Clerk, first published in London in 1961).

LETTERS TO MALCOLM: CHIEFLY ON PRAYER. New York: Harcourt, Brace and World, 1964.

THE DISCARDED IMAGE, An Introduction to Medieval and Renaissance Literature. Cambridge: The Cambridge University Press, 1964.

POEMS. Walter Hooper, ed. New York: Harcourt, Brace and World, 1965 (originally published in London in 1964).

STUDIES IN MEDIEVAL AND RENAISSANCE LITERATURE. Collected by Walter Hooper. Cambridge: Cambridge University Press, 1966.

LETTERS OF C. S. LEWIS. W. H. Lewis, ed. New York: Harcourt, Brace and World, Inc., 1966.

LETTERS TO AN AMERICAN LADY. Clyde S. Kilby, ed. Grand Rapids, Michigan: William B. Eerdmans Publishing Company, 1967.

SPENSER'S IMAGES OF LIFE. Alastair Fowler, ed. Cambridge: The University Press, 1967.

GOD IN THE DOCK, Essays on Theology and Ethics. Walter Hooper, ed. Grand Rapids, Michigan: William B. Eerdmans Publishing Company, 1970.

THE JOYFUL CHRISTIAN, 127 Readings from C. S. Lewis. New York: Macmillan Publishing Co., Inc., 1977.

THEY STAND TOGETHER, The Letters of C. S. Lewis to Arthur Greeves. Walter Hooper, ed. London: Collins, 1979.

THE BUSINESS OF HEAVEN. Walter Hooper, ed. New York: Harcourt, Brace, Jovanovich, 1984.

FIRST AND SECOND THINGS, ESSAYS ON THEOLOGY AND ETHICS. Walter Hooper, ed. London: Collins-Fount Paperbacks, 1985.

TIMELESS AT HEART, ESSAYS ON THEOLOGY. Walter Hooper, ed. London: Collins-Fount Paperbacks, 1987.

THE ESSENTIAL C. S. LEWIS. Lyle W. Dorsett, ed. New York: Macmillan Publishing Company, 1988.

LETTERS, C. S. LEWIS, DON GIOVANNI CALABRIA, A STUDY IN FRIENDSHIP. Translated and edited by Martin Moynihan. London: Collins, 1989.

ALL MY ROAD BEFORE ME: THE DIARY OF C. S. LEWIS 1922-1927. Edited by Walter Hooper. New York: Harcourt, Brace, Jovanovich, 1991.

B. Biblical Citations And Church Documents

NEW AMERICAN BIBLE. Nashville: Catholic Bible Press, 1987.

NEW REVISED STANDARD VERSION BIBLE. Division of Christian Education of the National Council of the Churches of Christ in the U.S.A., 1989.

VATICAN COUNCIL II — THE CONCILIAR AND POST-CONCILIAR DOCUMENTS. Austin Flannery, O.P., ed. Collegeville: Liturgical Press, 1981 Edition.

MARIALIS CULTUS — (DEVOTION TO THE BLESSED VIRGIN MARY). Apostolic Exhortation of Pope Paul VI. Washington, D.C.: United States Catholic Conference, 1974.

REDEMPTORIS MATER (MOTHER OF THE REDEEMER). Encyclical Letter by Pope John Paul II. Washington, D.C.: United States Catholic Conference, 1981.

MULIERIS DIGNITATEM (THE DIGNITY AND VOCATION OF WOMEN). Apostolic Letter of Pope John Paul II. Washington D.C.: United States Catholic Conference, 1988.

CATECHISM OF THE CATHOLIC CHURCH, Libreria Editrice Vaticana. New York: William H. Sadlier Inc., 1994.

C. Secondary Source Books And Commentaries

ALLCHIN, A.M. *The Joy of All Creation: An Anglican Meditation on the Place of Mary.* Cambridge, MA: Cowley, 1984.

ANDREWES, Lancelot. *The Devotions of Bishop Andrewes*. Transl. from the Greek and arr. by John Henry Newman. New York: G. H. Richmond and Co., 1897.

ANDREWES, Lancelot. *Private Prayers*, Hugh Martin, ed. London: SCM Press, 1957.

BARFIELD, Owen. *Owen Barfield on C. S. Lewis*. G. B. Tennyson, ed. Wesleyan University Press, 1989.

BARRAT, David. *C. S. Lewis and His World*. Grand Rapids, Michigan: Eerdmans, 1987.

BELLOC, Hilaire. *At the Sign of the Lion*. Freeport, New York: Books for Libraries, Inc., 1964.

BONAVENTURE, St. *The Soul's Journey into God, The Tree of Life, The Life of St. Francis* in *The Classics of Western Spirituality*. Ewert Cousins, Transl. New York: Paulist Press, 1978.

BUBY, Bertrand, S. M. *Mary, The Faithful Disciple*. Mahwah, New Jersey: Paulist Press, 1985.

_____. *Mary of Galilee*, Vol. I: Mary in the New Testament. New York: Alba House, 1994.

_____. *Mary of Galilee*, Vol. II: Woman of Israel — Daughter of Zion. New York: Alba House, 1995.

_____. *Mary of Galilee*, Vol. III: The Marian Heritage of the Early Church. New York: Alba House, 1997.

CAROL, Juniper B., O.F.M. (ed.) *Mariology*, Vol. I. Milwaukee: The Bruce Publishing Company, 1955.

CARPENTER, Humphrey. *The Inklings: C. S. Lewis, J.R.R. Tolkien, Charles Williams, and Their Friends*. Boston: Houghton Mifflin, 1979.

CHESTERTON, G. K. *The Everlasting Man*. New York: Dodd, Mead and Co., 1925.

_____. *Selected Essays of G. K. Chesterton*. Chosen by Dorothy Collins. London: Methuen, 1949.

COMO, James T., ed. *C. S. Lewis at the Breakfast Table and Other Reminiscences*. New York: Harcourt-Brace, 1992.

COREN, Michael. *The Man Who Created Narnia: The Story of C. S. Lewis*. Grand Rapids, Mich.: W. B. Eerdmans Pub., 1996.

DAVIES, Julian. *The Caroline Captivity of the Church*. Charles I and the Remoulding of Anglicanism, 1625-1641. Oxford: Clarendon Press, 1992.

DE LA POTTERIE, Ignace, S. J. *Mary in the Mystery of the Covenant*, transl. by Bertrand Buby, S. M. New York: Alba House, 1992.

DERRICK, Christopher. *C. S. Lewis and the Church of Rome*. San Francisco: Ignatius Press, 1981.

DORSETT, Lyle W. *And God Came In*. New York: Macmillan Publ., 1983.

_____, ed. *The Essential C. S. Lewis*. New York: Macmillan Publishing Company, 1988.

EVANS, G. R. and WRIGHT, J. Robert, eds. *The Anglican Tradition: A Handbook of Sources*. Minneapolis, MN: Fortress Press, 1991.

FITZMYER, Joseph A. *The Gospel According to Luke I-IX*. New York: Doubleday and company, Inc., 1981.

⎯⎯⎯⎯. *Luke the Theologian: Aspects of His Teaching*. New York: Paulist Press, 1989.

FORD, Paul F. *Companion to Narnia: A Complete Guide to the Enchanting World of C. S. Lewis's The Chronicles of Narnia*. San Francisco: Harper Collins Publishers, 1980.

FULLER, Edmund. *Myth, Allegory, and Gospel: an Interpretation of J.R.R. Tolkien, C. S. Lewis, G. K. Chesterton and Charles Williams*. Minneapolis: Bethany Fellowship, Inc., 1974.

GILBERT, Dougles R. *C. S. Lewis: Images of His World*. Grand Rapids, Michigan: Eerdmans, 1973.

GREEN, Roger Lancelyn and HOOPER, Walter. *C. S. Lewis — A Biography*. New York: Harcourt Brace Jovanovich, 1974.

GRESHAM, Douglas H. *Lenten Lands, My Childhood with Joy Davidman and C. S. Lewis*. New York: Macmillan Publishing Company, 1988.

GRIFFIN, William. *Clive Staples Lewis: A Dramatic Life*. San Francisco: Harper and Row, 1986.

GUMPEL, Peter and MOLINARI, Paolo. *Il Capitolo VI "De Religiosis" della Costituzione Dogmatica sulla Chiesa* in *Quaderni di Vita Consacrata*, Vol. 9. Milano: Editrice Ancora, 1985.

HERBERT, George. *The Country Parson* and *The Temple* in *The Classics of Western Spirituality*. John N. Wall, Jr., ed. New York: Paulist Press, 1981.

HOLMER, Paul L. *C. S. Lewis: The Shape of His Faith and Thought*. New York: Harper and Row Publishers, 1976.

HOOKER, Richard. *The Works of that Learned and Judicious Divine, Mr. Richard Hooker*, arr. by John Keble. Oxford: The University Press, 1845.

HOOPER, Walter. *C. S. Lewis: A Companion and Guide*. New York: Harper Collins Publishers, 1996.

HOWARD, Thomas. *C. S. Lewis: Man of Letters*, A Reading of His Fiction. San Francisco: Ignatius Press, 1987.

JELLY, Frederick M., O.P. *Madonna, Mary in the Catholic Tradition*. Huntington, Indiana: Our Sunday Visitor Publishing Division, 1986.

JOHN PAUL II, POPE. *Marian Reflections*, The Angelus Messages of Pope John Paul II. David O. Brown, O. S. M., ed. Washington, New Jersey: AMI Press, Inc., 1990.

KILBY, Clyde S. *Images of Salvation in the Fiction of C. S. Lewis*. Wheaton, Ill.: Harold Shaw Publishers, 1978.

———. *The Christian World of C. S. Lewis*. Abingdon, Berks.: Markham Manor Press, 1965.

KREEFT, Peter. *Making Sense Out Of Suffering*. Ann Arbor, Michigan: Servant Books, 1986.

———. *C. S. Lewis: A Critical Essay*. Front Royal, Virginia: Christendom College, 1988.

———. *Heaven*, The Heart's Deepest Longing. San Francisco: Ignatius Press, 1989.

———. *Back to Virtue*. San Francisco: Ignatius Press, 1992.

———. *Your Questions, God's Answers*. San Francisco: Ignatius Press, 1994.

_____. *The Shadowlands of C. S. Lewis*, The Man Behind the Movie. San Francisco: Ignatius Press, 1994.

_____. *C. S. Lewis for the Third Millenium*. San Francisco: Ignatius Press, 1994.

_____. *Angels (and Demons)*. San Francisco: Ingatius Press, 1995.

LANGLAND, William. *The Vision of Piers Plowman*. New York: Sheed and Ward, 1945.

LAO TZU. *Tao Te Ching*. Mair, V. H., transl. New York: Bantam, 1990.

LINDVALL, Terry. *Surprised by Laughter*, The Comic World of C. S. Lewis. Nashville, TN: Thomas Nelson Publ., 1996.

LOSSKY, Nicholas. *Lancelot Andrewes The Preacher (1555-1626)*, The Origins of the Mystical Theology of the Church of England. Oxford: Clarendon Press, 1991.

LOVASIK, Lawrence G. *Our Lady in Catholic Life*. New York: The Macmillan Co., 1957.

MACDONALD, George. *Phantastes, A Faerie Romance*. London: J. M. Dent and Sons Ltd.

MACQUARRIE, John. *Mary for all Christians*. Grand Rapids, Michigan: William B. Eerdmans Publishing Company, 1990.

MASCALL, Eric Lionel and BOX, H. S., eds. *The Blessed Virgin Mary: Essays by Anglican Writers*. London: Darton, Longman and Todd, 1963.

MCADOO, Henry R. *The Spirit of Anglicanism*, A Survey of Anglican Theological Method in the Seventeenth Century. New York: Charles Scribner's Sons, 1965.

MCHUGH, John. *The Mother of Jesus in the New Testament*. New York: Doubleday and Company, Inc., 1975.

MORNEAU, Robert F. "The Impact of Divine Love", Vol. 5 of an 8-Volume Cassette Series. New York: Alba House, 1990.

MORRICE, William. *Joy in the New Testament*. Grand Rapids: Eerdmans, 1984.

NEILL, Stephen. *Anglicanism*. Oxford: Mowbrays, 1977.

NEWMAN, John Henry. *Mary — The Second Eve*. Rockford, Illinois: TAN Books and Publishing, Inc., 1982.

NICHOLS, Aidan, O. P. *The Panther and the Hind*, A Theological History of Anglicanism. Edinburgh: T & T Clark, 1993.

NOCKLES, Peter Benedict. *The Oxford Movement in Context: Anglican High Churchmanship, 1760-1857*. Cambridge: Cambridge University Press, 1994.

O'CARROLL, Michael, C. S. Sp. *Theotokos*, A Theological Encyclopedia of the Blessed Virgin Mary. Collegeville: The Liturgical Press, 1982.

O'DONNELL, Christopher. *At Worship With Mary, A Pastoral and Theological Study*. Wilmington, DE: Michael Glazier, 1988.

O'MEARA, Thomas A. *Mary in Protestant and Catholic Theology*. New York: Sheed and Ward, 1966.

PACKER, John William. *The Transformation of Anglicanism*. Manchester: University of Manchester Press, 1969.

PATRICK, James & WALKER, Andrew, eds. *A Christian for All Christians*, Essays in Honor of C. S. Lewis. Washington: Regnery Gateway, 1992.

PICKERING, W. S. F. *Anglo-Catholicism: A Study in Religious Ambiguity*. London: Routledge, 1989.

RATZINGER, Joseph Cardinal. *Daughter Zion*. San Francisco: Ignatius Press, 1983.

RICHARD, Lucien. *Christ The Self-Emptying of God*. New York: Paulist Press, 1997.

ROBERTS, Alexander & DONALDSON, James, eds. *The Ante-Nicene Fathers*. Vol. I. Grand Rapids, Mich.: Wm. B. Eerdmans Publishing Co., 1973.

SAWARD, John. *Christ is the Answer*, The Christ-Centered Teaching of Pope John Paul II. New York: Alba House, 1995.

SAYER, George. *Jack, C. S. Lewis and His Times*. San Francisco: Harper and Row, 1988.

_____. *Jack: A Life of C. S. Lewis*. Westchester, Illinois: Crossway Books, 1994.

SAYERS, Dorothy L. *The Whimsical Christian*, 18 Essays. New York: Macmillan Publishing Company, 1978.

SCHEEBEN, M. J. *Mariology*. St. Louis: B. Herder Book Co., 1947.

SEMMELROTH, Otto, S. J. *Mary Archetype of the Church*. New York: Sheed and Ward, 1963.

SIBLEY, Brian. *C. S. Lewis Through the Shadowlands, The Story of His Life with Joy Davidman*. Grand Rapids, Michigan: Fleming H. Revell, 1985.

SIMCOX, Carroll E. *The Historical Road of Anglicanism*. Chicago: Henry Regnery Company, 1968.

TAMBASCO, Anthony J. *What Are They Saying About Mary?* New York: Paulist Press, 1984.

TAVARD, George H. *The Thousand Faces of the Virgin Mary*. Collegeville: The Liturgical Press, 1996.

TAYLOR, Jeremy. *The Rule and Exercises of Holy Dying*, Thomas S. Kepler, ed. Cleveland: World Pub. Co., 1952.

———. *Jeremy Taylor, Selected Works*, Thomas K. Carroll, ed. in *The Classics of Western Spirituality*. Mahwah: Paulist Press, 1990.

TREANOR, Oliver. *Mother of the Redeemer, Mother of the Redeemed*. Dublin: Four Courts Press, 1988.

TUVE, Rosemond. *Allegorical Imagery*. Princeton: Princeton University Press, 1966.

TYACKE, Nicholas. *Anti-Calvinists*, The Rise of English Arminianism c. 1590-1640. Oxford: Clarendon Press, 1987.

VANAUKEN, Sheldon. *A Severe Mercy*. San Francisco: Harper San Francisco, 1977.

———. *Under the Mercy*. San Francisco: Ignatius Press, 1985.

WEIGER, Josef. *Mary, Mother of Faith*. Chicago: Henry Regnery Company, 1959.

WILLIAMS, Charles. *Charles Williams: Essential Writings in Spirituality and Theology*, Charles Hefling, ed. Cambridge: Cowley Publications, 1993.

WILLIS, John Randolph. *Pleasures Forevermore: The Theology of C. S. Lewis*. Chicago: Loyola University Press, 1983.

WILSON, A. N. *C. S. Lewis: A Biography*. New York: Norton, 1990.

D. Dictionaries And Encyclopedias

BENET, William R., ed. *Benet's Third Edition Reader's Encyclopedia*. New York: Harper and Row Publishers, 1987.

CIRLOT, J. E. *A Dictionary of Symbols*. New York: Philosophical Library, Inc., 1962.

CROSS, F. L. & LIVINGSTONE, E. A., eds. *The Oxford Dictionary of the Christian Church*. Oxford: Oxford University Press, 1983.

FARRUGIA, Edward G., S. J. & O'COLLINS, Gerald, S. J. *A Concise Dictionary of Theology*. New York: Paulist Press, 1991.

O'CARROLL, Michael, C. S. Sp. *Theotokos: A Theological Encyclopedia of the Blessed Virgin Mary*. Collegeville, MN: The Liturgical Press, 1982.

SCOTT, A. F. *Current Literary Terms*, A Concise Dictionary. New York: St. Martin's Press, 1965.

E. Journal Articles

CLASPER, Paul. "C. S. Lewis and the Ministry of Spiritual Direction" in *Review for Religious*. Vol. 48. Mr-Ap 1989, pp. 264-76.

COUSINS, Ewert H. "Bonaventure, the Coincidence of Opposites and Nicholas of Cusa" in *Studies Honoring Ignatius Charles Brady Friar Minor*. Theology Series No. 6.St. Bonaventure, N.Y.: The Franciscan Institute, 1976, pp. 177-97.

DERRICK, Christopher. "Some Personal Memories of C. S. Lewis, an Incarnational Man" in *New Oxford Review*. Vol. 54. Nov., 1987, pp. 16-20.

FERNANDEZ, Irene. "C. S. Lewis on Joy" in *Communio*. Fall, 1982, pp. 247-57.

HOOPER, Walter & MALLON, J. "From Lewis to Hooper to Rome" in *Crisis*. Vol. 12. Jl-Ag, 1994, pp. 34-38.

HOWARD, Thomas. "The Cult of C. S. Lewis" in *Crisis*. Vol. 12. Jl-Ag, 1994, pp. 28-29.

IMBELLI, Robert. "Screwtape Revisited" in *America*. Vol. 151. Nov. 17, 1984, p. 324.

JACOBS, Alan. "The Second Coming of C. S. Lewis" in *First Things*. No. 47. Nov., 1994, pp. 27-30.

KUNG, Hans and MOLTMANN, Jurgen, eds. "Mary in the Churches" in *Concilium*. Vol. 168. Oct., 1983.

KREEFT, Peter J. "Friends of the Faith: C. S. Lewis: the Century's Finest Apologist" in *National Catholic Register*. Vol. 66. Ja 28, 1990, pp. 1ff.

_____. "A Trialogue with C. S. Lewis, Martin Luther, and Thomas Aquinas" in *New Oxford Review*. Vol. 61. Jl-Ag, 1994, pp. 5-16.

MEILAENDER, Gilbert. "Psychoanalizing C. S. Lewis" in *The Christian Century*. Vol. 107. May 16-23, 1990, pp. 525-29.

MORNEAU, Robert F. "Letters of Gratitude" in *Review for Religious*. Vol. 46. My-Je, 1987, pp. 429-40.

ROSSOW, Francis C. "Giving Christian Doctrine a New Translation: Selected Examples from the Novels of C. S. Lewis" in *Concordia Journal*. Vol. 21. Jy, 1995, pp. 281-97.

SELLNER, Edward C. "C. S. Lewis as Spiritual Mentor" Vol. 14. Sept., 1984, pp. 21-3.

SPRINGER, Kevin. "In Search of Joy" in *New Covenant*. Vol. 14. Sept., 1984, pp. 21-3.

STEBBINS, Madeleine F. "50th Anniversary of the Conversion of Our Founder" in *Lay Witness*. Vol. 17, no. 4. May, 1996, pp. 13-15.

VANAUKEN, Sheldon. "Let us Stand Together" in *Crisis*. Vol. 11. Ja, 1993, pp. 47-8.

_____. "Old Western Man: C. S. Lewis and the Old South (and other dinosaurs)" in *Crisis*. Vol. 11. Dec., 1993, pp. 26-30.

WOOD, Ralph C. "The Baptized Imagination: C. S. Lewis's Fictional Apologetics" in *Christian Century*. Vol. 112. Ag 30-Sep 6, 1995, pp. 812-15.

VII — An Anglo-American Literary Review publ. by the Marion E. Wade Center of Wheaton Coll. (Wheaton, Ill.), Vols. 11 (1994) & 12 (1995).

Mary in Faith and Life in the New Age of the Church. Proceedings of the "Marian Seminar 1980" of the International Marian Research Institute. Publ. By Franciscan Mission Press (Ndola — Zambia), 1983.

F. Published Dissertations

BOYER, Steven Dwight. *Authority in the Theological Vision of C. S. Lewis*. Ph.D. Thesis. Boston University, 1996.

DESCHENE, James Michael. *Joy in a Minor Key: The Mystery of Gender and Sex in the Thought of C. S. Lewis*. Ph.D. Thesis. University of Rhode Island, 1991.

FORD, Paul Francis. *C. S. Lewis, Ecumenical Spiritual Director: A Study of His Experience and Theology of Prayer and Discernment in the Process of Becoming a Self.* Ph.D. Thesis. Fuller Theological Semiary, School of Theology, 1987.

HENTHORNE, Susan Casandra. *The Image of Woman in the Fiction of C. S. Lewis*. Ph.D. Thesis. State University of New York at Buffalo, 1985.

HUGHES, Larry Raymond. *The World View of C. S. Lewis Implicit in His Religious Writings*. Ed.D. Thesis. Oklahoma State University, 1980.

KNIGHT, Bettie Jo. *Paradise Retained: "Perelandra" as Epic*. Ph.D. Thesis. Oklahoma State University, 1983.

MARTIN, Robert Edwin. *Myth and Icon: The Cosmology of C. S. Lewis' "Space Trilogy"*. Ph.D. Thesis. The Florida State University, 1991.

MATTHEWS, Kenneth Ernest. *C. S. Lewis and the Modern World (England)*. Ph.D. Thesis. University of California at Los Angeles, 1983.

NOLAN, Mary Catherine. O. P. *The Magnificat, Canticle of a Liberated People*. S.T.D. Thesis. International Marian Research Institute, 1994.

SAUDERS, Paulette G. *The Idea of Love in the Writings of C. S. Lewis*. Ph.D. Thesis. Ball State University, 1987.